T0067406

HOW TO DEVELOP
PROFESSIONAL SELLING SKILLS & TECHNIQUES

Based on Common Sense & Ethics

By Anthony J. Danna

Order this book online at www.trafford.com
or email orders@trafford.com

Most Trafford titles are also available at major online book retailers.

© Copyright 2017 Anthony J. Danna.
All rights reserved. No part of this publication may be reproduced, stored in a retrieval
system, or transmitted, in any form or by any means, electronic, mechanical, photocopying,
recording, or otherwise, without the written prior permission of the author.

Print information available on the last page.

ISBN: 978-1-4120-4043-3 (sc)

Because of the dynamic nature of the Internet, any web addresses or links contained in
this book may have changed since publication and may no longer be valid. The views
expressed in this work are solely those of the author and do not necessarily reflect the
views of the publisher, and the publisher hereby disclaims any responsibility for them.

Any people depicted in stock imagery provided by Thinkstock are models,
and such images are being used for illustrative purposes only.
Certain stock imagery © Thinkstock.

Trafford rev. 03/17/2017

www.trafford.com
North America & international
toll-free: 1 888 232 4444 (USA & Canada)
fax: 812 355 4082

DEDICATION

TO MY PARENTS TONY & Sally and my sister Kathleen, who by their teaching and example, provided me with a solid foundation and grounding on the principles of character, integrity, respect, fairness, courage, confidence and moral values.

To the many members of the Danna family who gave me the opportunity and safe environment to observe and learn how to put these principles into practice.

To my Business College Professors at York College and Penn State University who professionally taught me the detailed principles of Business Administration.

To my mentor and most important College Professor, Mr. Charles Seligman of York College, who patiently taught me how to study and learn business principles and whose methods I still use today and have taught to many salespeople nationwide.

To my many professional sales managers and sales colleagues with whom I have been privileged to work with over 45 years and who have taken the time to share their successful sales techniques with me.

To all salespeople who are striving to reach a higher level of professional selling based on Common Sense and Ethics.

TABLE OF CONTENTS

DEDICATION. iii

ACKNOWLEDGMENTS xi

FORWORD xiii

PREFACE xv

INTRODUCTION xix

<u>SELLING ESSENTIALS</u>

<u>PART ONE:</u>

Preparation, Prospecting And Making Appointments. 1

Chapter 1:   Preparation. 3
Chapter 2:   Prospecting. 7
                    Why Must You Prospect: 7
                    Where To Prospect: 8
                    How To Prospect: .8
                    You Have Found A Prospect Whom Will Talk
                    With You. 11
Chapter 3:   Making Appointments 13
                    Once you have found a prospect what should
                    you do next? 13
                    Making Appointments: 13
Chapter 4:   How To Meet With A Prospect Who Is
                    Difficult To Reach 15
Chapter 5:   Strive To Be The First Vendor To Respond: 17

PART TWO:

Conducting Sales Calls – A Sample Sales Cycle. 21

Chapter 6:   Step 1 Of The Sales Call – Meeting With
                   Your Customer Or Prospect. 23

Chapter 7:   Step 2 Of The Sales Call – Qualifying And
                   Fact Finding. 25
                   Determining A Prospect's Level Of Satisfaction
                   With Their Existing Service Provider: 28

Chapter 8:   Step 3 Of The Sales Call – Determining Pros-
                   pect's Objectives, Needs, Desires, Issues
                   And Problems That Need To Be Resolved . . .33
                   Listening: 35

Chapter 9:   Step 4 Of The Sales Call –
                   Presenting The Benefits And
                   Features Of Your Products Or Services. 37

Chapter 10:   Step 5 Of The Sales Call – Discuss And Define
                   What The Next Steps Are To Be In The "Sales
                   Cycle". 39
                   Action Items To Be Determined:. 39
                   Summarize:. 40
                   At The Conclusion Of The First Meeting
                   With A Prospect:. .40

PART THREE:

Professional Selling Techniques, Strategies And Scenarios 41

Chapter 11:   Handling Questions And Objections. 43
                   Handling Questions:. 43
                   Handling Objections: 44

Chapter 12:   Conducting Corporate Tours, Product
                   Demonstrations And Customer Site Visits. . .47
                   Corporate Tours:. 48
                   Product Demonstrations: 48
                   Customer Site Visits:. 50
                   Refreshments: 51
                   Your Post Corporate Tours And Product Demon-
                   stration Duties:. .51
                   Your Post Customer Site Visit and Product
                   Demonstration Duties:. 52

Chapter 13:   Proposal Preparation, Strategy And
Presentation: 61
Proposal Preparation: Benefits Of Taking Extra
Time To Prepare A Proposal:. 61
Proposal Strategy: 62
Proposal Presentation Techniques:. 63

Chapter 14:   Price Changes And Sales Promotions. 67

Chapter 15:   Having Breakfasts/Luncheons/Dinners With
Accounts. 69

Chapter 16:   Keeping In Contact With Prospects
During A Lull In The Sales And
Decision Making Cycle 71
When lulls occur during a sales cycle, I recom-
mend that you also consider the following
additional techniques:. 73

Chapter 17:   Requests For Information (RFI), Requests For
Proposals (RFP's) And Requests For Quotes
(RFQ's): 75

PART FOUR:
Buying Signals, Trial Closing, Closing And Negotiations. 81

Chapter 18:   Buying Signals 83
Verbal Buying Signals:. 83
Non-Verbal Buying Signals: 84

Chapter 19:   Trial Closing. 87
What Is Trial Closing?. 87
When Should You Trial-close? 87
Why Should You Trial-close?. 87
General Trial Closing Questions:. 88
Specific Trial Closing Questions:. 89

Chapter 20:   Closing The Sale - Asking For The Order. . . .91
Pre-Closing Techniques: 91
Sample Questions To Illustrate Pre-Closing
Tecniques:. 91
Customized Pre-Closing Questions: 92
Closing Techniques. .93
Asking For The Order: 93

Chapter 21:   Negotiations. 97

PART FIVE:

Post Sale Wins And Losses And Having Patience 99

Chapter 22:   Post Sale - Wins 101
Chapter 23:   Post Sale - Losses .105
Chapter 24:   Having Patience 109

PART SIX:

Your Career And Your Sales Manager 111

Chapter 25:   What To Do When Things Are Not Going Well
                 In Your Sales Career .113
Chapter 26:   Your Sales Manager 115
Summary Of Chapters 1 Through 26 – "Selling Essentials" 117

THE SECRETS OF SELLING

Chapter 27:   Trust Your Instincts and Intuition 123
Chapter 28:   Price-checkers. 127
                 Additional Signs That Indicate You Are
                 Dealing With A Price-Checker: 129
                 Additional Information Regarding
                 Price-Checkers: 131
                 Excusing Yourself From Price-checking Sales
                 Scenarios: 133
                 Advantages Of Purposely Working With
                 Price-Checkers: 134
Chapter 29:   Non-Verbal Body Language 137
Chapter 30:   Interruptions Are Your Friends, Keep The Sales
                 Process SIMPLE, Think BIG 139
                 Interruptions Are Your Friends: 139
                 Keep The Sales Process SIMPLE: 140
                 Think BIG: 140
Chapter 31:   Relationship Selling And Consultative Selling. . .143
                 Relationship Selling: .143
                 Consultative Selling: .145
                 Developing Mentors: .145
                 Dressing For Success: .146
Chapter 32:   What To Do When Problems Arise In Your
                 Account After The Sale. 149

What To Do When Problems Arise In Your
Account After The Sale:. 149
What To Do When You Lose Your Key
Contact In An Account: 150
Competitive Considerations:. 151

The Secrets Of Professional Salespeople

Chapter 33:   Revealing The 120 Fundamental Secrets Of
Professional Salespeople. 153

Summary. 171

ACKNOWLEDGMENTS

TO MY DAUGHTER MICHELLE RIEHL for the many hours she invested in editing this book.

To Len Marrella whose character, ethics, moral values, professionalism, advice and guidance provided the inspiration that made this book possible.

To Dennis McClellan for his preliminary review and evaluation of my manuscript and encouragement to pursue publication of this book.

To Fred Mogel, Fred Myers and Sanford Piltch for their continued wise counsel, guidance and support.

To my father-in-law Virgil Hellrung and college instructor Charles Seligman whose lives were examples of impeccable character and integrity. Their friendship, influence and mentoring are deeply missed.

To my close friends, confidants and colleagues Rich Brucker, Joe Fasano, Rick Mitchell, Whip Overmiller, Archie Sybrandt and Andy Zacherl whose character and values are of the highest standards. Our friendships continue to last throughout the years and their support, insights, wisdom and sound advice are always trusted and valued.

To the many fine salespeople, sales managers, sales instructors and sales support staff with whom I have had the privilege to work with and learn from. I am especially indebted to those sales professionals who have taken the time to teach me the fundamentals of their common sense approach to selling. I have also been fortunate to observe and learn many of their professional, ethical selling techniques and human relations skills.

FOREWORD

EFFECTIVE SALESMANSHIP IS SIMILAR TO effective friendships, effective marriages and effective relationships. Effective selling like effective leading is built on trust. And trustworthiness is best served as an outgrowth of our shared values. Living our values is one of the most effective ways to develop long-term positive relationships and long-term positive relationships are of paramount importance for permanent and continuing success in selling.

The values that are so important for developing long-term sales success are the same as values we hold dear in other successful relationships – values such as honesty, responsibility, fairness, compassion and respect for the dignity of every human being. When you have achieved all of the above you have only fulfilled one half of the equation – the character element.

To be completely effective as a sales person, one also needs to develop good sales skill and techniques – which is the competence half of the equation. So there you have it. Character and competence are necessary ingredients for effective leaders – and the same equation works wonders for sales people.

As a sales person, Tony Danna has lived this equation of competence and character and he is the type of sales person you want to do business with time and time again. In this book he has, in a common sense way, outlined everything you need to know to be successful – and probably happy too. I think you will like the journey.

> Len Marella, DBA
> President
> Center for Leadership and Ethics

PREFACE

EVERYONE IS IN SALES! YOU do not have to be a salesperson to be in sales. You can be in the accounting, purchasing, inventory control or customer service departments, and still be part of a sales team. We are all still in sales!

After being in the sales profession for over 45 years, which included being a National Sales Training Instructor, why did I choose to write this book now? I began to realize that most of the effective selling and human relations techniques that I have learned have come from the knowledge I have acquired in the real world of selling. I also continue to learn and use new successful selling techniques. Granted, there are many sales training courses and books to read, all of which are important and helpful towards becoming a successful salesperson. However, I did not learn the finer points of selling from the sales training courses I have attended, or books I have read. I learned these enhanced techniques in the trenches, and feel it is now time to share this knowledge with individuals interested in advancing their skills in the sales profession.

This book is intended to make you aware of the advanced techniques of how to become a professional salesperson. With these techniques you will be able to attain a higher level of professionalism, confidence, enthusiasm and success when selling. You will also be able to separate yourself as a true sales professional from the crowded field of other capable sales people in your line of business.

My objective is to pass along the knowledge and insights that I have acquired throughout my years of real world selling.

This book identifies common selling mistakes and how to avoid them. This book will also reveal to you the many proven, successful selling techniques that I have learned and developed over the years.

Another purpose of this book is to present guidelines on how to develop, practice and implement techniques for professional selling based on **common sense** and **ethics**.

Using a **common sense** approach towards selling will build upon the fact that becoming a successful salesperson involves maintaining a positive frame of mind. It has to do with how you think. It has to do with how you approach selling in your mind and place trust in your intuition. A successful salesperson's two most valuable assets are their mind and their time.

Ethics is presented as a key approach. Ethics is such an important topic that I felt the need to instruct salespeople on how to professionally develop and earn their customer's confidence and trust based on ethical business practices. This book will present information and examples on how to develop professional selling skills based on ethical standards. These standards will relate directly to your moral character. The strength of you character will be based on your ability to develop and adhere to high moral standards and principles that will help to set you apart from other salespeople.

The information and insights in this book are candid, straightforward, realistic and in focus. They are presented in a condensed form so that they can be easily remembered, referred to and applied on a daily basis. These chapters are designed to be easily read, digested and implemented by the reader. The brevity of some chapters is intended to appeal to people seeking real world, practical, no-nonsense answers to making themselves better salespeople and, therefore, making their sales team more effective.

I do want to attest to the fact that the examples and scenarios presented in this book are based on actual events and circumstances that I have personally experienced. Some you will find interesting, enlightening and thought provoking. Others you will find truly unique! You will ask yourself if some of these implausible scenarios are really true. Do they actually occur in the real world of selling? The answer is yes! This is another reason why I felt this book needed to be written. I want other aspiring professional salespeople to know and be aware that many different and unpredictable situations do exist in the sales world. Sales professionals need to always expect the unexpected.

It is my goal that you will find many of the suggestions, techniques and strategies presented in this book helpful and applicable for your daily use towards successful selling. They can be applied when you are selling yourself, your company, your company's products/services or your own ideas. They can be used when selling to your business prospects, customers, your corporate management team, intra- or inter-departmental co-worker teams or even members of your family.

This book is meant to present a practical approach to the profession of selling. I will review how to develop and maintain a positive attitude and how to turn a lost sale into a learning experience. I will demonstrate how to take sales situations with little potential and use these as opportunities to develop and practice new sales techniques.

I have found that the techniques, strategies and insights presented have worked successfully. Hopefully, they will be of benefit to you and help you towards becoming a professional salesperson.

INTRODUCTION

THIS BOOK HAS BEEN WRITTEN for both the novice as well as the seasoned salesperson. This book is divided into two sections. In the first section I will present "**Selling Essentials.** " In the second section the focus will be on the "**Secrets Of Selling.**"

"**Selling Essentials**" reviews basic selling techniques and strategies for the outside "business-to-business" salesperson so they can broaden their existing sales skills. Specific nuances within each step of the sales process will be presented which will reveal many interesting, successful and proven selling techniques. Many of the selling techniques and suggestions presented can also be used by inside sales staff, customer service staff or any corporate personnel who have direct customer contact. These same techniques can also be applied by many internal departmental and management personnel when they are selling and presenting new ideas, proposals, projects, plans or reports to other internal staff members.

With "**Selling Essentials**" we will review basic selling techniques of how to:

- Prepare
- Prospect
- Make appointments
- Conduct sales calls
- Meet with your customer or prospect
- Qualify and fact find
- Determine prospect's objectives, needs, desires and issues

- Present the benefits of your company's products or services
- Handle questions and objections
- Conduct corporate tours, product demonstrations and customer site visits
- Prepare and present proposals
- Recognize buying signals
- Trial-close, asking for the order and closing the sale
- Negotiate

This second part of this book will focus on the **"Secrets Of Selling."** In this section, we will build upon the foundation of "Selling Essentials" in order to further develop your selling skills. I will present many special insights into successful selling methods and techniques that will help very good salespeople to become exceptional, professional salespeople. These will be the salespeople who can separate themselves from the crowd of competitors and sell successfully at a much higher level of professionalism. These insights are not usually found in textbooks or presented in sales training classes. They have been learned on the job after many successful years of experience. You will also learn many secrets and techniques on how to develop your selling talents by weaving common sense and ethical approaches into your own personalized **art form** of selling!

The **"Secrets Of Selling"** will focus on the following topics:

- Trusting your instincts and intuition
- Price-Checkers
- Non-verbal body language
- Why interruptions are your friends
- Keeping the sales process SIMPLE
- Thinking BIG
- Relationship and consultative selling
- Developing Mentors and Dressing For Success
- Problems arising in accounts
- Loosing a key contact in an account
- Competitive Considerations
- Revealing The 120 Fundamental Secrets of Professional Salespeople

Throughout this book the terms **prospect, account, customer,** and **client** will be used. For purposes of clarification, use of the terms **prospect or account** will denote a person or company who is currently not doing business with you. The terms **customer or client** will denote a person or company who is currently doing business with you, but is presenting you with a new sales opportunity. These terms will be used randomly throughout this book and always in the context that you are *selling* to them. The use of these terms is not intended to denote any specific difference in how you are to approach your sales opportunity. These terms are also used randomly because when you are *selling* to someone, the intent is that you should be able to use the same techniques and methods presented in this book for all opportunities. Also, the terms **vendor, supplier, product** or **service provider** will be used to denote you and your competitors as salespeople.

Finally, this book and all of the guidelines presented are based on common sense and ethics. I have written this book to help you further your career as a professional salesperson. I encourage you to always keep the selling process SIMPLE. Be honest and ethical in all of your business dealings and your customers will trust and respect you as a *consultative* salesperson. My goal with this book is to present a framework of helpful selling methods, strategies, techniques and insights in a logical order. In this way, these suggestions can be easily utilized, brought forward naturally and applied whenever they are needed, in whatever sequence needed. Remember, no matter what we do, we are **all** in sales!

SELLING ESSENTIALS
PART ONE:
PREPARATION, PROSPECTING AND MAKING APPOINTMENTS

CHAPTER ONE
PREPARATION

WHATEVER YOU DO IN LIFE you should always prepare ahead of time for the event. Whether this means going on a vacation, doing odd-jobs around your home or just getting ready for work, you should prepare and make all the necessary arrangements so that your venture will be successful.

Preparation is a key element in whatever career choice or business endeavor you choose. When pursuing a career in sales, how does a professional salesperson prepare for selling? What are the little things they do that produce success in the long run? The following are suggestions on how to adequately prepare for selling. These suggestions are applicable for the business-to-business outside salesperson as well as the inside salesperson.

- Fuel your sales vehicle the night before in order to not waste time doing so in the morning

- Lay out your next day's schedule the night before. Note and prioritize calls to be made, administrative duties to be performed, projects that need follow-up, proposals to be developed, corporate and customer meetings that you will be attending. This activity can be done on a weekly or monthly basis as well.

- Whether driving to meet prospective clients or calling them on the telephone, develop your prospecting schedule days or weeks ahead of time.

- Always keep a copy of your personal schedule with you and available so you can make appointments quickly.
- Before meeting with a prospect:
  - Be sure of the names and titles of the prospect's key staff members.
  - Understand their roles and responsibilities within the organization.
  - Prepare your thoughts and plan of how you wish to conduct the meeting.
  - Make sure all presentation materials are in the correct order.
  - Make sure you bring all brochures you plan to leave with the prospect.
  - Prepare notes on the important issues and needs you want to address or create.
  - Have accurate directions on how to reach your prospect's office.
  - Know approximately how long it should take you to reach your prospect's office.
- During the meeting:
  - Verify the names, spelling and pronunciation of the prospect's key staff members.
  - Have all fact-finding questions you plan to ask written down.
  - Execute your plan on how you want to conduct the meeting.
  - Be flexible to rearrange or change these plans on a moments notice.
  - Refer to your prepared notes on the important issues and needs you want to address or create.
  - When the prospect is giving you important information, make sure you take notes.
- Be prepared to handle objections and relate your product or service features as benefits to the account.
- If your products and services are not able to meet a prospect's needs, be honest and admit this immediately. This is the ethical thing to do. However, this can also be a situation for you to be creative and

flexible. This is where you begin to sell on a consultative level. We will review consultative selling in **Chapter 31**.

- Redefine your prospect's needs. Make sure you know exactly what issues these needs will resolve and the benefits to be realized by your prospect. Next, discuss alternative solutions and approaches provided by your products and services that can truthfully meet or even exceed the prospect's initial needs.

- You can also create different, valid needs that can be resolved by your products and services. These resolvable needs may minimize or eliminate your prospect's original needs. You may even provide solutions to additional issues that the prospect had not considered.

- At the conclusion of the meeting, have a plan of what you would like to have happen next, but be flexible to do what the prospect wants to accomplish next. Also, review all the notes you have taken with the prospect. This is to make sure you have recorded all the important information correctly and that each of you know who is responsible to do what before your next meeting.

Preparation requires self-discipline and consistency. Self-discipline is an important character trait that you must develop to consistently prepare for each prospect meeting. This level of preparation must become part of your normal daily sales routine. By doing so you will always demonstrate to your accounts that you are well-prepared, confident and ready to conduct your sales call. This will also help to build your prospect's confidence and trust in you.

When conducting a meeting or making a sales presentation, preparation can make a significant difference in your level of professionalism. You will be more relaxed knowing that you have a basic plan of what needs to be accomplished, what questions you plan to ask, what product benefits you expect to present, etc.

Preparation will also enable you to concentrate more on:

- Interacting with your prospect.
- Answering their questions.
- Creating and discovering issues and needs.
- Developing valid innovative and creative solutions to their needs.
- Reading their body language and recognizing what their reactions are telling you.

- Staying on track when interruptions occur.

Becoming a successful salesperson has to do with how you **think**. How you approach selling is in your **mind**. How you use your **mind** and **thought processes** will enable you to focus yourself to learn and utilize the right sales tools and techniques at the right time. **Remember, becoming a successful professional salesperson is all in your mind!**

CHAPTER TWO

PROSPECTING

Why Must You Prospect:

P ROSPECTING MUST BE DONE IN order to find qualified potential customers. Trying to live off your established customer base by selling only to them is usually not the best business decision. It is not a practical approach towards selling. A successful salesperson is always looking for new sales opportunities. Bringing in new business is the lifeblood of any salesperson and necessary for the survival of a company. Plus, you can be assured that your competition is always looking for new business.

Let me get right to the point. Most salespeople do not like to prospect. The reality is that successful salespeople **have to** prospect! Some companies have the luxury of a business development department. However, your level of success as a professional salesperson is ultimately your responsibility. In order to achieve your level of desired success, you will have to do some level of prospecting on you own. You must learn to depend on yourself, not others.

In order to prospect, you must get yourself in a positive frame of mind. You have to accept prospecting as part of your job as a professional sales-person. You must realize that there are new accounts out there that need your help and can benefit from your products and services. Once you have properly prepared yourself, prospecting can actually be an enjoyable duty. You can also view prospecting as a means of taking a break from your regular selling routine and a refreshing change of pace. You will meet new accounts, new people, solve new customer needs and build a portfolio of potential new accounts. If you actively prospect on a regular basis, you always will have a profitable backlog of potential new business, which will keep you energized. Plus, when you review all of the accounts you sold, you will become aware of how many of these sales came about because you prospected and you found the lead on your own!

Where To Prospect:

Next, to begin prospecting you must clearly have your territory identified, whether it be geographic, line of business, size of customer or whatever designations your company uses to define sales territories. Never infringe on another salesperson's territory. If situations arise where there is an issue, discuss the matter immediately with your manager and your colleague. The goal is arrive at an **ethical** and **equitable** resolution. You must demonstrate your honesty and truthfulness to not only your accounts, but also to your colleagues. People must know that your character is such that you can be depended upon to be a person of integrity and high moral values.

When you have been assigned to a territory, one of the first things you should do is personally visit each of your existing customers. By doing this you can meet and establish a business relationship with each of your accounts. They will get to know you and who they can call regarding any needs or questions they may have. There may also be potential sales opportunities within these existing accounts. People will buy from people who they know, like, trust and can, therefore, help them meet their needs. People will be buying from you, not your company.

How To Prospect:

There are many ways to prospect. As reviewed earlier, you must always be actively prospecting on your own. In addition, some companies utilize a telemarketing service to generate sales leads. Other companies use business development staff that do more research and investigative work to develop more qualified sales leads. This staff may also send out introductory letters and corporate information to potential customers.

Lead generation networks are also formed by business development staff working together with their peers who are in different companies, but in similar industries (e.g., building and construction). These types of networks are loosely organized and their business activities and interactions ebb and flow based on business or economic conditions.

Business professionals that represent different companies or occupations form other lead generation organizations. These groups do business in the same geographic trading area, but conflicts of interest are not allowed. Only one company can represent each type of business or occupation and, therefore, members cannot be in competition with each other. These types of groups are very organized, have bylaws and meet on a regular basis. They will have members whose business relationships span many years regardless of business or economic conditions. Organizations such as these can be the most beneficial type of lead generation groups to join.

Corporate office parks are another viable method of prospecting. Potential tenants for corporate office parks will have many questions for managers of these parks. Managers of office parks will usually provide information packets to their prospective tenants. Ask these managers if they would agree to include information about your company, products and services in these information packets. Some managers may be reluctant, but others may be willing to include your information. If your corporate material enhances their information packets and possibly enables these managers to attract tenants, you may be on your way toward developing very profitable business relationships.

The following are additional methods and ideas on how to prospect for new accounts for your products or services:

- When personally meeting with your customers, ask if they can refer you any other accounts.

- Join and become active in local service organizations that compliment the products or services you sell.

- Join and become active in your local Chamber Of Commerce or Business/Manufacture associations.

- Obtain lists of potential accounts for your sales territory.

- Obtain lists of your company's current accounts as well as those of your competitors'.

- If you are an authorized dealer for products, ask the manufacturer if they can provide account lists in your territory.

- Obtain reports that indicate companies that may be moving.

- Obtain reports that indicate companies that may be building a new facility or expanding their existing facilities.

- Subscribe to local County Planning Commission Land Development Reports.

- Watch for new construction or building additions while you are driving. Ask your family members and friends to let you know if they see any similar type of activity in their travels.

- Study Standard Industry Classification (SIC) Code reports. These reports, which are localized by geographic areas, categorize all business by a line of business classification code.

- Read local line of business directories. (e.g., Manufactures, Wholesale Distributors, Building Contractors, Electrical Mechanical Contractors, Architects, Engineers, Attorneys, etc.) Again, consider joining and becoming an active member in organizations that compliment the product or services you represent.

- Subscribe to Local Trade or Business Journals.

- Read your local newspapers: Business, Classified, Legal, Local sections, etc.

- Develop business relationships with other sales people who represent non-competitive products and services and call on the same types of accounts as you.

- Position yourself to be a subcontractor for other companies that can use your products or services for their prospects. These companies can then use your pricing when they respond to bids.

- Examine the Yellow Pages of your local telephone book.

- Inquire among your friends, family relations and professional business associates who work for other companies.

- Participate in Trade Shows. (e.g., Line of Business Trade Shows, Local Chamber of Commerce Seminars and Business Expos, etc.)

- Use the Internet and it's wealth of information. Harness the power, productivity and flexibility including the many available applications, tools and search engines.

Whenever your list of active prospects is decreasing or business slows down for whatever reason, examine your prospecting methods to make sure that you are following your proven productive routines. Perhaps you have to make some adjustments or become more creative and innovative. However, it is possible that you just have to stay on course, stay focused and continue using your proven prospecting skills to work through periods of slow activity.

Always keep accurate records on prospects. A slow time in business activity can also afford you an opportunity to go back through and review your old prospecting records and contact these accounts. You may find a few old prospective accounts that may now be in a position to make a buying decision.

You Have Found A Prospect Whom Will Talk With You.

As a result of prospecting, you have found an account with a key person willing to talk with you. At this time you must have a brief, professional, polished introduction ready. This introduction must state who you and your company are, what your company does and how your products and services may be of benefit to their operations. Your goal is to secure a 15-minute to a half-hour audience with them to learn more about their corporate operations and needs.

At this crucial time you need to quickly pique their interest. You have to be able to identify and briefly discuss some important industry specific needs that are common to the prospect's business. With any luck the prospect may state their needs or you may have to create a need in their mind for your products and services. You may also want to state that you are already helping many companies in their area. Mentioning a few of your well-known accounts will always help. You may even want to reference one or two of the prospects' competitors who are benefiting from your products and services! You can usually expect to get some kind of reaction with this last technique.

CHAPTER THREE
MAKING APPOINTMENTS

Once you have found a prospect what should you do next?

ACT QUICKLY! MAKE APPOINTMENTS TO visit them as soon as possible after you have made contact. If they do not want a visit, but just want some preliminary pricing or information about your company, products or services, provide them with this information quickly. Mail, fax, email or personally drop off the information quickly with a promise as to when you plan to follow-up. If you do not move with haste, your competitors may reach the account ahead of you. Remember, they are also prospecting. Plus, you must always assume that the account is working with their existing vendor and may already be in contact with other competitive vendors.

Making Appointments:

When making appointments with accounts, your goal should be to accommodate both their time frame and yours. I recommend you first ask the account, "What are the best times for you to meet? Early in the morning, after lunch or late afternoon?" When they answer this question, offer them two time frames that suit your schedule. If these times are not satisfactory for the account, immediately give them control and ask for times that suit them. Your goal is to secure an appointment! Although your time is valuable, ultimately you must be considerate and meet when it is convenient for the account. You should take your time frame into consideration with the account only if you already have prior appointments with other accounts or personal commitments that cannot be changed.

When asking for an appointment, let the prospect know how long a meeting time you will be requesting. If you ask for 45 minutes and the account cannot give you this much time, suggest 30 or 15-minutes. As a professional salesperson, you have to be flexible enough to pack all of your important information into a sales call that may last only 10 or 15-minutes.

Be **respectful** of an account's time. If they have agreed to a 15 or 30-minute meeting and this time has expired, remind them that the agreed upon time frame has ended. Ask if they would like to continue the meeting now or schedule another appointment. Usually the account will ask you to continue. However, you must give them the opportunity to decide. They will also appreciate your honesty and consideration for their time and that you can be relied upon to honor your agreements.

For prospects that have a very busy schedule, request appointments on the quarter hour (e.g., 8:15am, 9:45am, etc.). Requesting appointments on the quarter hour indicates to your prospect that you do not want to take-up much of their time. This method works best when you are only requesting a 15-minute meeting to introduce yourself and your company.

Be cognizant of the fact that certain accounts may prefer to meet with vendors at times that are much better than others. Some accounts prefer to meet first thing in the morning, right after lunch or late in the afternoon. There are other accounts whose best time to meet may be early in the morning or later in the evening. Early in the morning can be 6:30am or 7:00am! Later in the evening can be 6:30pm - 7:00pm or later.

Some accounts may not be able to meet with you between 8:00am and 5:00pm. If so, ask them what time is the earliest or latest you can meet. Usually they will hesitate for a moment. This is when you can suggest "how about 7:30 in the morning or 5:30 in the evening?" Then be quiet. Wait for their response. They will normally reply with a time that is suitable for them. The end result is that you will have achieved your goal of obtaining an audience with the account during non-standard business hours.

For early morning, noontime or later evening meetings, you may want to consider inviting the account to breakfast, lunch or dinner. If so, please review the information in **Chapter 15: Having Breakfasts/Luncheons/Dinners With Accounts.**

CHAPTER FOUR

How To Meet With A Prospect Who Is Difficult To Reach

THERE HAVE BEEN TIMES WHEN I've located an account that I've deemed a good prospect, but I could not make contact with the key person. This was because I either could not get past the *gatekeepers* of their schedule, or the person was just too busy to be approached during normal business hours. I recommend three techniques to overcome this issue.

The first is to call or visit their office at 7:00am to 7:30am or at 5:30pm to 6:00pm! Why? Because the *gatekeepers* are usually not on duty at these times! You can walk right in the front door and ask the first person you meet if the key person you want to meet is available. You may find that they will escort you right to this person. If you are calling on the telephone, ask to be transferred to the key person. Usually anyone answering the telephone at these hours is not a *screener* and they may do as you have requested. Also, in a sole proprietorship company, the owner is very likely the person who will answer your call during non-business hours.

The second recommended technique is to visit the account's site around mid-morning on Saturdays. This technique works best for family run or sole proprietorship accounts.

Try these first two techniques. You may be pleased to find the key decision makers that you seek are on the job during these non-standard business hours.

The third is to correspond with the key person via a fax, email or send them a good old-fashioned introductory letter! When mailing introductory letters, you can also enclose more information about your company as well as brochures regarding your products and services. I personally have had the best luck with introductory letters or faxes because it puts a hard copy document in their hands. Plus, now you have a legitimate reason to make follow-up telephone calls to the key contact to verify they have received the material you have sent.

When you follow-up and are greeted by the *gatekeepers* who are *screening* your call, you can ethically tell them who you are and that you are following-up on information you have sent to their supervisor. Chances are that the *gatekeepers* will not be able to quickly dismiss you. Especially if they have no idea what it is you have sent. If they do ask what the material is in reference to, have a very important, honest and forthright description or explanation of what your material is about. Do not try to be coy or deceptive. This will not be well received. The goal is for them to have to put you on hold too check-in with their supervisor. With any luck you will be able to talk with the key person.

CHAPTER FIVE

STRIVE TO BE THE FIRST VENDOR TO RESPOND

Y OU MUST STRIVE TO BE the first vendor to respond to a prospect's interest or inquiry. This enables you to set the standards for the sales campaign and control the sales cycle.

You should always strive to be **first** in an account in order to:

- Personally visit the account.

- Determine if they are truly a prospect.

- Listen to and analyze their existing needs.

- Position yourself as a reputable sales consultant.

- Mention a few of your satisfied accounts. Especially if they are in this prospect's same line of business

- Position yourself as consultant who will analyze their needs and custom design a solution for their particular needs.

- Create additional valid needs and issues that the prospect should be aware of that can be resolved by and are favorable to your company and products. Qualify the prospect to make sure they agree that these additional needs and issues are now important and your solutions would be of benefit to them. (**Please reference Chapter 19: Trial Closing.**)

- Position the unique and specific benefits of your company - products, services or support that your competition will have difficulty in matching. Again, qualify the prospect to ensure that they agree that these benefits are also important to them. (*Trial Close*)

- Combine the prospect's valid existing and additional created needs and issues along with the unique and specific solutions you can provide. Again, re-affirm that they are important for the prospect and seek agreement from them.

- Answer prospect's questions honestly. If you do not know the answer, assure the prospect that you will get the answer promptly. It is OK if you do not have all the answers immediately. Many prospects do not expect you to have answers to all of their questions immediately. Especially if they are technical in nature.

- Promptly provide the prospect with information they need, request or that you have promised to provide.

- If necessary, conduct necessary research and report back to the account as soon as possible. If the research is taking longer than anticipated, stay in constant contact with the account and let them know of your progress.

- Demonstrate or present your products or services.

- Invite them to visit your corporate offices.

- Develop and present pricing options.

You will usually be in a favorable position with the prospect if your competitors tend to respond slowly or if the account has to call them to ask for their information. Your goal is to be perceived by the prospect as a dependable, trustworthy person of character who responds in a timely manner and is sincerely interested and anxious to do business with them.

Following these techniques of how to control a sales cycle will enable you to present a strong proposal and sound business case as to why the account should trust you and your company. Your goal is for the account to want to do business with you not your competition. By practicing these proven methods, you will find that many of your customers will want to *buy* from you rather than you having to *sell* them.

In the above information I have referred to *Trial Closing*. Trial closing is a very important qualifying technique of questioning a prospect to determine if they are still truly interested in your products and services. When *Trial*

Closing, you should seek agreement from the prospect that the solutions you are presenting are still important and of benefit to them and their operations. The trial closing technique helps you to affirm that your prospect is still willing to consider doing business with you and your company.

Trial closing also enables you to learn from a prospect if their original needs remain unchanged, have expanded or have been replaced or influenced by other issues. The goal is for their answers to be yes. If their answers are no, you must determine why. Did their needs change? Are there additional factors present that are influencing or changing their requirements? If so, you must develop a plan of action to address these new criteria to your prospect's satisfaction.

We will study trial closing in more detail in **Part Four - Chapter 19: Trial Closing**.

SELLING ESSENTIALS
PART TWO:
CONDUCTING SALES CALLS –
A SAMPLE SALES CYCLE

THIS SECTION WILL REVIEW THE fundamental steps of a sample sales cycle. However, events can occur that are completely out of your control that can speed up or slow down a sales cycle. Furthermore, your prospect usually will have a plan as to how they intend to shop for or investigate products or services they need. Their plan can completely rearrange how you intended the sales campaign to develop or how the specific sequences of a sales cycle may occur. Plus, depending on what products or services you sell, a sales cycle can last anywhere from a few minutes to a few years!

Therefore, when fact finding with your prospect, you must make sure you understand the sequence of the key details and factors that they need to experience in order for them to make a buying decision. You must always remain flexible, adaptable and ready to adjust your plans to accommodate the prospect whenever necessary. You must also always keep and open mind, be open to the possibilities, be prepared to "think outside the box" and be ready to adjust to different situations as they develop. **Remember, being a successful salesperson has to do with how you think and approach selling. Being a successful professional salesperson is all in your mind!**

Finally, be aware that every prospect and sales situation is different. As a professional, ethical salesperson, you must maintain the confidence that you can meet these distinct opportunities with a positive frame of mind. Plus, you should enjoy addressing all the different challenges and find that working with all the different personalities you will encounter is a rewarding experience. If done professionally, you can even produce reference lists of your customers who had previously been serviced by your competitors, but are now your accounts.

CHAPTER SIX

STEP 1 OF THE SALES CALL – MEETING WITH YOUR CUSTOMER OR PROSPECT

THE MAIN PURPOSE OF THIS first meeting is to establish rapport with the account. When meeting with a prospect for the first time, be prepared to introduce yourself, your company and what it is you have to offer and how it will be of benefit to them. Keep the introduction brief, smooth and professional.

When you are meeting with your prospect for the first time, you should strive to solidify your prospect's comfort level, trust and confidence in you, your company and your products or services. You can offer references and/or testimonial letters from satisfied customers preferably in the same line of business as your prospect. Your goal should be to differentiate yourself and your company from your competitors. Present the added value you have to offer versus your competition. You should also discuss and present supporting material documenting:

- The length of time your company has been in business serving and supporting local customers.

- Any honors or special recognition your company has received.

- Specific accomplishments your company has achieved.

- Your company's financial stability and reputation.

- Significant problems your company has solved for your customers.

- General features and functionality of your products, services and support and how these offerings have been of benefit and value to other accounts.

- The breadth of your product line.

- Your company's services and support guarantees.

- Technical certifications of staff.

When meeting with an account always use their name when speaking to them. The best sound anyone can hear is their name!

Never comment on the prospect's family pictures in their office. The same goes for trophies, awards or any other sort of memorabilia they have in their office. All the other salespeople before you have probably already done so. The prospect will know that your comments are not genuine. As an "ice-breaker," the only time you may want to consider commenting on hobby related items in an office is only if you are truly interested or enjoy the same hobby. Even then, keep it short and get down to business.

CHAPTER SEVEN
STEP 2 OF THE SALES CALL – QUALIFYING AND FACT FINDING

WHEN MEETING WITH AN ACCOUNT for the first time there are two distinct types of overall qualifying and fact-finding questions you should be asking. The first of these are general leading questions that would pertain to almost all businesses or life situations. The second types of questions are those that are specific to each type of company's industry/line of business marketplace. You will have to develop your specific trade questions yourself. The purpose of this chapter is to focus on general leading questions in order to fact find and qualify.

Asking leading questions will encourage your prospect to give you more discussion oriented and detailed answers versus just yes or no answers. The goal is for you to use these types of questions as guidelines to develop your own specific questions for your particular selling marketplace.

As you may already realize, every prospect is different. They each will have different needs and their own preferred way of moving forward and deciding what, when, where, why and how they make buying decisions. The prospect will also normally already have defined who are the decision makers and which staff influence and make recommendations to the ultimate decision maker. The challenge for the salesperson is to figure this all out and put this selling puzzle together for each individual prospect in the their context while you are selling your products or services. The following are examples of types of qualifying questions to ask in order to determine if you are dealing with a valid prospect.

The examples presented are general leading, fact-finding and qualifying questions you can use with any prospect. These questions are based on who, what, when, where, why and how type of questioning approach. For example:

1. Who is their current service provider?

2. How satisfied is your prospect with their existing service provider? If the prospect is satisfied, proceed cautiously by asking more qualifying questions. If the prospect is dissatisfied, ask if them to detail their areas dissatisfaction in order to determine whether they are still willing to do business with their existing service provider.

3. How open is your prospect and their management team to changing product or service providers?

4. Would they be willing to consider alternate providers or solution methods for their business needs?

5. Do they have a preferred vendor they are favoring at this time? Whether the answer is yes or no, ask them why?

6. How satisfied is your prospect with their existing operations? Are they open to considering the benefits of the products or services you offer?

7. What is your prospect doing now to accomplish whatever task your product of service can embellish?

8. When will a decision be made to consider changing providers or current solution methods in place?

9. What will be your overall decision time frame? (This question is to help you judge the length of your sales campaign.)

10. Are you in an active decision making mode now or are you just gathering information?

11. Why are you considering making changes in your operations at this time?

12. What are your plans for this year? Next year? The next five or ten years?

13. Where do you envision your company's direction in the next few years?

14. How do you plan to grow your company over the next few years?

15. What is the short-term vision for your company?

16. What is the long-term vision for your company?

17. What has changed in your business in the last 5 or 10 years?

18. How does your approach to business differ from your competitors?

19. What are your greatest challenges/opportunities?

20. What do you need to do to generate more business?

21. What are some expected events for which you have to be prepared?

22. What are some opportunities that for which you could take advantage?

23. What strategic initiatives are you pursuing to position your company for the future?

24. What are your long-term dreams for your company?

25. How many facilities do you have? Where are they located?

26. How many more facilities do you plan to open (or close) in the next few years?

27. Are you considering making acquisitions? Are you considering selling any of your operations or facilities?

28. Who are the ultimate decision makers that determine whether or not to make a change to new products or services?

29. Who are the other key staff personnel that should be involved because they influence the ultimate decision? Do these people influence a decision or can they actually recommend whether or not to buy or change vendors?

30. How much money do you have budgeted for the project? (It always helps if the prospect has the money to buy your product or service!)

31. What are the decision-making criteria to be used when selecting a vendor?

32. What exactly do you have to do to win their business? The prospect should provide you with satisfactory answers.

33. Verify and qualify the prospect by asking them that, if you can successfully meet their needs (e. g. questions #1 through #5 and #21

through #25 above), will they seriously consider doing business with you? Again, the prospect should provide you with a straightforward satisfactory answer. If not, you may be dealing with a *"price-checker."* (Please reference **"The Secrets Of Selling" Chapter 28: Price-Checkers**)

Trust your common sense and intuition. If things do not seem right, they probably are not right. Remember, the prospect does have an ethical duty to convince you that their intentions to give you a fair opportunity to win their business are honorable. Unfortunately, not all prospects adhere to this moral standard. If you are not satisfied with answers to your questions, it may be because you sense that the prospect may not be willing or able to do business with you. If so, trust your instincts. It may be best for you to move on and find another prospect.

Determining A Prospect's Level Of Satisfaction With Their Existing Service Provider:

This paragraph is a further discussion of **question #2 above**.

If the prospect states that they are satisfied with their existing service provider, ask them as to why they are satisfied. Ask what aspects of the incumbent vendor's products, services and support that they are most pleased with and why.

Determine if your product and service offerings are superior to your competitor's and can you position them as such with the prospect. Determine if the prospect is truly open to considering your company as a viable alternative. Ask the prospect why they want to consider having you present a bid for their business. If they have invited you to meet with them, ask what is it that interests them in your company's products and service offerings. Why would they want to consider doing business with you? Why do they want to consider alternative vendors? Finally, what is it you must do in order to win their business?

If the prospect states that they are not satisfied with their existing service provider, ask them as to exactly why they are not pleased. Ask what are the reasons and circumstances for their dissatisfaction. What is their level of dissatisfaction?

Is it slight, moderate or high where they absolutely must and want to make a change of vendors?

If the prospect is not satisfied, ask the question if there is anything their existing vendor can or will be doing to alleviate their level of dissatisfaction. If the answer is yes, then refer to the first paragraph previously discussed above to determine that if their existing vendor makes any changes and improvements, will the prospect be willing to continue doing business with their vendor.

If the answer to the question is no, that the existing vendor will not be making any changes, ask that in the event this vendor does decide to make last minute changes or improvements to their products or services, presents lower pricing than other bidders or offers giveaways, guarantees, etc., would the prospect still be willing to continue doing business with them. If the prospect's answer is no, then you must now qualify and trial close your prospect on the fact that they are so dissatisfied with their current vendor, that they will not consider any other factors as reasons to stay with their current vendor. Your objective in this scenario is to obtain an affirmative answer, which is yes; they do want to make a change. At this point you may have a valid prospect. You can now begin to fact find to determine your prospect's objectives, needs, desires, issues and problems that need to be resolved. Details of this step of the sales cycle are presented in **Chapter 8**.

It is fair to say that prospects may or may not agree to give you accurate, detailed information regarding the above qualifying scenarios. However, you must try to get these questions answered in order for you to know and understand exactly what type of prospects you are dealing with and if they represent an opportunity that warrants your time and effort. There are prospects that may be satisfied with their current vendor, but are also genuinely seeking alternative options and vendors. These types of prospects can also be considered valid prospects. As presented in **question #22 above**, you must also go through this same exercise of qualifying questions when you meet other key decisions makers. This will further enable you to determine whether or not you are dealing with a "*price-checking*" opportunity.

Additional Important Qualifying Questions:

- Is their budget based on a calendar or fiscal year? This will tell you when they can make a buying decision.

- Do they have any money budgeted? This will tell you if they can and are planning to make a purchase.

- Do they prefer to purchase or make time payments? Will they need any type of special terms or conditions in your sales agreement?

Answers to these questions may facilitate your being able to present different procurement options.

If you sell equipment, you can ask if they prefer brand new, factory reconditioned or used equipment? In addition to a purchase price, would they also like pricing on renting or leasing? If you sell services, you can ask if they want the basic, standard or deluxe package of services. These are very interesting and important questions because they can enable you to give the prospect several options to buy from you vs. your competition who may only propose one option.

There are many other questions that can be asked. The above are just a few samples of leading questions to ask that will encourage prospects to communicate with you. This will enable you to learn more about their needs, wants, future plans and ability to make a buying decision. With answers to key questions you will begin to learn how you may want to structure and conduct your sales campaign. These key questions are:

- Who are the decision makers, influencers and recommenders?
- Is the account satisfied with their current operations?
- Are they satisfied with their current service provider?
- Is the prospect willing and open to making a change in vendors?
- Are they in an active decision making mode right now?
- Does the prospect have the money budgeted to make a buying decision now?

By obtaining answers to these questions, you will be able to make an intelligent initial decision as to whether or not you are dealing with a valid, qualified prospect. You can also determine if you will have an opportunity to be of service to them now or in the future. The goal of the above-suggested questions is to pre-qualify your prospect. Your objective is to decide if you can be successful in conducting a sales campaign, presenting a proposal and ultimately closing a sale with a qualified prospect.

Always take a step back to examine and analyze each sales opportunity. Use your common sense to determine if the account is being honest and up front with you. Again, trust your instincts.

If you cannot neutralize or render unimportant a specific prospect's need (s) for which you do not have a solution, it is best to address this honestly, up-front and early in the sales cycle. If the needs or issues in question are "deal breakers" and you cannot meet these needs, it is best to stop pursuing the opportunity. It only takes one important prospect issue or need that you cannot satisfy for you to lose a sale. Conversely, it only takes one important prospect issue or need that only you can legitimately provide for you to win a sale.

Make sure you are confident you can meet or exceed all of the prospect's needs. If you cannot, be honest with yourself and your prospect. Tell them that you cannot meet their needs and suggest that it is in their best interest that you do not pursue this sales opportunity. If the prospect does want you to continue, you must have them agree and commit that the issues in question must be completely removed from their decision making process and will not be revisited by them later in the sales cycle. Even if they agree, be realistic with yourself and decide if the opportunity is worth pursuing. It is better to have no prospect than a prospect that you do not have a reasonable chance of selling. **Time is your greatest asset. You must guard and protect it and use it wisely!**

CHAPTER EIGHT

STEP 3 OF THE SALES CALL – DETERMINING PROSPECT'S OBJECTIVES, NEEDS, DESIRES, ISSUES AND PROBLEMS THAT NEED TO BE RESOLVED

WHETHER YOU ARE MEETING WITH a prospect for the first time or conducting subsequent meetings, you must always strive to determine their objectives, needs, desires, issues and problems that need to be addressed. Ask questions.

Be sincerely interested in determining your account's needs and issues. They will realize and be appreciative that you are genuinely trying to help them. Work hard to determine which of your company's products, services and related features and benefits can resolve their issues and provide the necessary solutions for the prospect.

Become proficient in understanding the benefits and features of your products or services and how to position them to meet or exceed your prospect's objectives. Know your key product or service advantages and how they provide value-added solutions to your prospect's needs and objectives. Know which of your advantages will give you and your prospect a competitive edge.

Integrate and weave your company's products and services with related benefits and features into productive, solution oriented sales calls.

Uncover additional legitimate hidden issues! Hidden issues are ones that the prospect should have for their line of business, but they are just not aware that they exist. An additional sales technique is to create valid new issues! These issues are the types you uncover that are very unique to the way the individual prospect operates their business. Seek agreement with the prospect that they need to resolve these hidden or new issues. Your goal should be to create new prospect issues and needs that only the features of your products and services can address and resolve.

As a professional consultative salesperson, you must strive to relate the prospect's objectives and needs along with your product or service features to provide the prospect with the solutions and benefits they will realize by agreeing to do business with you and your company.

The following are just some of the key concepts that are at the heart of every business purchase decision. Learn how to fold these into your benefit statements.

- Increase Revenue and Decrease Costs
- Improve Corporate Image, Productivity and Efficiency
- Generate Cost Savings
- Improve Corporate Stability, Return On Investment
- Increase Capacity
- Add Value To Overall Corporate Operations
- Encourage Growth
- Increase Level Of Customer Service and Support
- Increase Market Share
- Increase Level Of Customer Satisfaction
- Improve Morale
- Lower Cost Of Ownership
- Satisfy Needs and Objectives
- Improve Competitiveness in the Marketplace.

Listening:

Above all, listen to what your prospect is saying to you. Be genuinely interested in what they are saying. Do not interrupt them when they are answering your questions. Take notes. Even when you are hearing their needs and you know that you have the exact solution to their needs. Be patient. Let the prospect talk. Ask more questions.

Keep listening. Take more notes. If you are a good listener, the prospect will tell you exactly what they want and need and just what you need to do to sell them. You will have ample time in **Step 4** of the sales call to present your solutions that will be of benefit to your prospect. **The best conversationalists are people who actually say little, but are very good listeners!**

CHAPTER NINE

STEP 4 OF THE SALES CALL – PRESENTING THE BENEFITS AND FEATURES OF YOUR PRODUCTS OR SERVICES

DURING THIS FIRST SALES CALL your goal is to have your prospect identify their future goals as well as their current objectives, needs, desires, issues and problems. The next step is for you to present your company's solutions and their related benefits to address not only the current prospect's needs and objectives, but also their future aspirations.

When introducing the features of your product or service solutions, you must add value and differentiate them from your competition. You should consider doing the following:

- Stress your product or service advantages and the benefits they will provide to your account.

- Qualify and trial close the account as to how each advantage or feature of your product line will solve their needs.

- Seek their agreement and trial close early and often during this process.

- Concentrate on explaining the added value your products and services will give to your prospect. Especially emphasize the benefits that you can professionally posture as significant competitive advantages, consequently accenting competitor's weaknesses. By this I do not mean to blatantly point out competitor's weaknesses. Doing so would be unprofessional and unethical.

- In the course of sales calls, you should be emphasizing the strengths of your significant advantages. Rarely discuss your competitor's products or services during your sale. The prospect wants to hear about you and your company. Your purpose is to lay-out the foundation upon which you will be building your own customized sales campaign for this account. The goal is that when your competitors are presenting their solutions to the account, you will want them to fall short of the solutions and benefits offered by your company.

- Proactively present your weaknesses known by your competitors as advantages to the account. This technique diffuses the competition's sales plan to use your weaknesses against you and will help you maintain control of the selling process.

- When making subsequent visits to the account, keep on emphasizing your solutions and their advantages.

- Emphasize the competitive edge your solutions and advantages will provide the account over their competition.

- Emphasize the better service and support the account will be able to deliver to their customers that will increase the level of their customer's satisfaction.

- Never underestimate the intelligence of accounts. Accounts will usually realize the difference in advantages between you and your competition on their own.

- You must continue to qualify, seek agreement and trial close throughout this entire process.

CHAPTER TEN

STEP 5 OF THE SALES CALL – DISCUSS AND DEFINE WHAT THE NEXT STEPS ARE TO BE IN THE "SALES CYCLE"

YOU ARE NOW AT THE point in the first sales call with your prospect where you have decided that they are a qualified prospect. you have determined their needs and objectives, sought agreement and successfully trial closed them on the benefits and features of your products and services. Now what do you do? The following are suggestions on preparation for the next meeting with the prospect.

Action Items To Be Determined:

- What are you to do next?
- What does your prospect want you to do next?
- What is your customer or prospect to do next?
- Clearly define and assign these action items to each other.
- Establish a time-line.
- Seek Agreement.
- Schedule the next meeting.

Summarize:

- Re-state and summarize the results of your fact finding.

- Ensure that all of your prospect's needs, issues and concerns have been addressed.

- Qualify and seek agreement regarding the benefits that your specific products or services will provide to this prospect.

- Agree on who is to do what and the time frame for completion before the next meeting.

- Continue to qualify, seek agreement and trial close with the prospect.

At The Conclusion Of The First Meeting With A Prospect:

Sincerely thank the prospect for the time they have spent with you and for the information they have provided. Make sure you have brought your corporate overview documents as well as product and service brochures that you can leave behind. **Highlight information in these handouts with a marker so the account does not have to hunt for the significant data. Enclose this information in oversize professional folders so as to increase your chances that the folder will not be misplaced.**

Be ready to develop legitimate reasons as to why you have to return for the next meeting. Agree upon the time frame and make a specific appointment as to when you both are to meet again. The more time you can spend in front of a prospect for valid reasons correlates directly towards increasing your chances of closing the sale. **Be prepared to continue to leave behind additional sales literature or information about your company in more folders after all visits. The more you can keep your company's name in front of a prospect, the more they will think of you and realize that you genuinely want their business.**

This is especially true when you have had to spend a considerable amount of time developing a relationship with and designing a solution for your prospect. If they are pleased with your work, pressed for time and have confidence in you and respect your character, they may very well decide to not spend much time with your competition and just place their order with you.

SELLING ESSENTIALS

PART THREE

PROFESSIONAL SELLING TECHNIQUES, STRATEGIES AND SCENARIOS

CHAPTER ELEVEN

HANDLING QUESTIONS AND OBJECTIONS

Handling Questions:

WHEN ASKED QUESTIONS BY PROSPECTS, there are two things you may consider doing before you answer their question. First, restate the question to make sure you understand exactly what the customer is asking. This also buys you time to begin to formulate your answer.

Secondly, if you are not sure of the nature of the question, ask the prospect to clarify or define more specifically why they are asking the question or what does this question mean to them. By following these two steps, you will learn that many times what the prospect is asking is something totally different than what you perceived they meant when you originally heard the question.

When you present your answer, try to relate the objective of their question to the features and advantages of the products or services you offer. This is an ideal opportunity to explain to the prospect the benefits they well realize by doing business with you.

Handling Objections:

Welcome objections! They indicate that the prospect:

- Is paying attention and listening to you.

- Is relating what you are presenting to their needs and objectives.

- Is interested in buying from someone.

Be attentive and respectful to all objections presented by an account. Never discount their importance. When an account offers objections, it does not necessarily mean that they are not interested in your products or services. They just may not understand what you are presenting. Their objection gives you an opportunity to ask them more questions and further explain and clearly define your subject matter. You can also offer the prospect more details as to your company or supplying vendor's approach to the topic at hand. If you feel that you have successfully answered and dealt with the objection, verify with the prospect that they are in agreement with your information.

Sometimes a prospect will be coached by the competition to present you with objections that are meant to accentuate your weaknesses as disadvantages. Turn these perceived weaknesses and disadvantages into advantages to the prospect. This can be accomplished by honestly and skillfully explaining why your company or supplying vendor has decided to approach certain issues the way they do. Further discuss why your existing accounts have found your company's approach to be of benefit to them. Mention some of these accounts by name. Competitors resorting to these tactics usually are regarding your company as a formidable competitor.

What if a prospect presents valid objections that you cannot overcome, explain or satisfy in any way? When this occurs, note the objections and ask if you can address them later. If the prospect agrees, continue on with your sales call. By using this technique, it gives you an opportunity to present all of the other benefits and advantages your prospect can experience by doing business with you. This extra time may render the objection unimportant or irrelevant. Also, you may gain enough additional information to successfully address their objection.

If the objections are still present and cannot be remedied, you must honestly tell the account that your product or service will not be able to meet their needs. Next, ask the prospect if these objections are "deal breakers". If they ask "what does this mean?", explain that you want to know if they feel they cannot or will not do business with you because of these obstacles that you cannot overcome. If their answer is yes, simply close your sales portfolio, push your chair back, thank them for their time and prepare to leave. In some cases you will be asked not to leave! If so, you may be in a much stronger position to make the sale than you had originally perceived.

This technique of handling objections indicates to the prospect that you honestly and ethically cannot provide them what they are claiming they need and you are prepared to abandon the sales effort. However, it also uncovers if the apparent insurmountable objections being presented are real or not.

Sometimes accounts will present objections that are smoke screens for other hidden objections. If so, once the account knows that you are finished meeting with them, cannot overcome these objections and ready to leave, they may ask you to stay and will reveal the true objections. I have had other cases where accounts purposely keep presenting objections until you finally cannot overcome one or more. This tactic seems to satisfy them that you are truthfully doing all you can for them.

When the prospect asks you to stay, you must trial-close them on the fact that there is no way you can overcome their objections. You must also trial-close them on the fact that if you continue consulting with them, they must agree to not raise this objection at the end of the sales process. They must agree to take this objection off the table here and now. If they agree, push your chair back to the table and reopen your sales portfolio! For one account I had to use this technique three times in two sales calls. They were getting used to me closing my sales portfolio and pushing my chair back! As it turned out, all of their insurmountable objections were smoke screens for the fact that they really wanted to do business with my company and me.

In the above scenario, the use of this technique of handling of objections can uncover the fact that you may be in a strong position to win their business. You just did not know this fact and the account was not willing to let you walk away. The advantages and benefits of your products and services must be of utmost importance to them. The prospect must also feel you have significant advantages over your competition that you can now begin to uncover.

On the flip side, if the account lets you leave, just leave. You used your common sense and instincts to determine that you did not have a valid prospect. You determined that you were not going to win their business anyway, so why waste their time and yours. Your time is valuable. Go find another prospect. Sometimes it is better to have no prospects than prospects that will not or cannot do business with you!

CHAPTER TWELVE

CONDUCTING CORPORATE TOURS, PRODUCT DEMONSTRATIONS AND CUSTOMER SITE VISITS

THIS IS ONE OF THE most exciting and key steps of the sales cycle. A corporate tour is when you have your prospect visit your office. During this time you will have their undivided attention to promote all aspects of your company and demonstrate your products.

It is very important that you show your prospect the brick and mortar of your company. You need to show them that you have a physical presence and commitment in their trading area. You now have an opportunity to demonstrate your products and physically show the prospect exactly how these products can be of benefit to them. Plus, you can also introduce your prospect to all of your support staff.

Preparation is key to every successful corporate tour and demonstration. Showing them your local branch office or worldwide corporate headquarters and demonstrating the specific solutions you have proposed will leave a lasting professional impression.

The following are the steps on how to arrange for a tour of your corporate offices and demonstrations of your products.

Corporate Tours:

- Decide upon a mutually acceptable date.

- Develop an agenda with the specific time, place and duration of each phase of the tour.

- Have your prospect agree with this agenda. (**Please See Sample Agendas at the end of this chapter.**)

- Personally visit the manager of each department who will be part of your tour and review the agenda with them. In this way, they will know where the prospect has been before arriving at their department and where the prospect will be going afterwards.

- Prepare each departmental manager with individual background information on each prospect attending the tour, their company's line of business, what each prospect wants to achieve by touring your manager's department and corporate facilities.

- Prepare each departmental manager with exactly what you want them present to each of your prospects. Make sure these managers know exactly what needs to be said and shown to your prospect in order to meet their needs and accomplish your sales objectives.

- Kick-Off Presentation: Have someone on corporate staff give a brief overview presentation on your company.

- Departments to visit: Customer Service, Help Desk, Sales Support, Technical Support, Engineering, Product Managers, Product Development/R&D, Marketing Department, Executive Offices, etc.

Product Demonstrations:

- If you plan to demonstrate products, review the same above information with those who will be helping you with the demonstrations.

- Review and practice all aspects of the demonstrations with your demonstration team at least one or two days before the prospect is to arrive. You need to allot time to make sure everything works before the prospect arrives!

- Keep the demonstrations SIMPLE and straightforward. Show the prospect exactly what they need to see.

- Try to do as much of the demonstration yourself. This gives your prospect confidence in you because you know your product.

- Most prospects do not expect to see a flawless demonstration. If you make a mistake during a demonstration, keep the situation light-hearted. This is really an opportunity for you to show the prospect how easy it is to correct an error when using your product. In some demonstrations I have even told my prospect that I was going to make a mistake on purpose just to show them how easy it is to recover from the error.

- Get the prospect involved with the demonstration. Have them get their *hands-on* the product and even assist you in conducting the demonstration. This will give them confidence in your product as well as themselves.

- Stay focused during your demonstration. Do not become distracted by questions or unexpected equipment difficulties. If questions occur, answer them. Readily admit if you do not have an answer, but assure the account that you will get the answer for them in a timely manner. If equipment problems occur, either fix them immediately or move on to the next phase of your demonstration. Address equipment problem areas later in the demonstration or avoid even trying to demonstrate known problem areas altogether.

- Have a colleague attend your demonstration to either assist or at least watch the interaction between the prospects and alert you to developments that you would normally miss. The purpose of this technique is for your colleague to be your extra pair of eyes and ears to help you throughout the demonstration. Also, make sure you enthusiastically reciprocate when your colleague has their prospects in for demonstrations.

- Have your product specialists on stand by and available to assist you during the demonstration.

- Have your product specialists actually demonstrate their areas of product expertise to the prospect. This proves to the prospect that sales support is available.

- It is OK to show a prospect some your product's other capabilities as long as they are meaningful to the prospect's needs. Do not show features that have no meaning to your prospect no matter how *whiz-bang* they may be. You may inadvertently confuse the prospect or create other needless issues that you now have to address. Also, do not get fancy and come up with any spur of the moment great demonstration ideas unless you are absolutely sure they will work and are meaningful to your prospect. If the great idea is untested and it does not work, it may ruin your entire demonstration efforts. This one issue alone has ruined many fine demonstrations.

Customer Site Visits:

For demonstration scenarios that involve taking a prospect to one of your company's satisfied existing customer sites, I recommended you follow all of the guidelines presented above for **Corporate Tours** and **Product Demonstrations.** The big difference is now you will have your customer actively involved in a tour of their facilities and you can depend on them to do their very best to demonstrate the products or discuss the services they have purchased from your company.

Other considerations, techniques and advice regarding customer site visits:

- A customer site visit is a very powerful way to present your products or services because not only are you showing your prospect your proven solutions in a live environment, they are also being presented and validated by a satisfied customer.

- Give each customer contact individual background information on each prospect attending the visit.

- Provide your customer with information about the prospect's line of business and what each prospect wants to achieve by visiting your customer's company.

- Prepare each customer contact with exactly you want them to present to each of your prospects. Make sure your customer knows exactly what needs to be said and shown to your prospect in order to meet the prospect's needs and accomplish your sales objectives.

- If possible, pick your account up at their office and drive them to your customer's site. On the way, you will have additional time to be with your account to not only review what they will be experiencing, but to also discuss the results of the customer visit on the way back to their office. Essentially, this technique enables you to have more one-on-one *selling time* with the account as well as the opportunity to build your *personal relationship* with them.

- Another technique is to begin with a **Corporate Tour** and **Product Demonstration** with your product experts at your office and then finish your day with a visit to an existing **Customer Site**.

Refreshments:

- Have refreshments such coffee, tea or even soft drinks available for your prospect if they will be visiting your office in the morning (e.g., 8:30 or 9:00am). You may even ask them ahead of time if they like pastries. If so, then have pastries available. You should learn your prospect's favorite types of refreshment or pastry and have these available for them. This can be a good lighthearted way to begin your event.

- If your prospect is visiting your office in the afternoon, usually just refreshments are adequate.

- If you are taking your prospect to a customer's office for a site visit, make any necessary arrangements for refreshments ahead of time with your account.

Your Post Corporate Tours And Product Demonstration Duties:

- Personally visit and thank each departmental manager, product specialist and corporate staff who assisted you in the tour and demonstrations. Give them an update as to the success of the prospect's visit.

- Next, write a general internal memo or email to all above staff personnel. Again, thank them for helping and also copy-in their managers. Thank you memos go a long way towards securing their help for your next prospect visit.

- Write a formal, personalized thank you letter to each prospect who attended the tour and demonstrations. This is also a good opportunity to provide them with any follow-up information they requested during their visit. (**Please See Sample Letters at the end of this chapter.**)

- When you win the business, write another general internal memo or email to the above staff personnel. Again express your appreciation and praise everyone for all their help in securing this new business and also copy-in their managers.

- Finally, when you win the business, have your corporate management team write a thank you letter to each attendee indicating how much they appreciate their business and their confidence in your company. **(Please see sample letters at the end of Chapter 22: Post Sale – Wins With Sample Letters)**

Your Post Customer Site Visit and Product Demonstration Duties:

- Personally call or visit your main customer contact that hosted your prospect's visit to their site. Give them an update as to the success of the prospect's visit.

- Write a formal, personalized thank you letter to your host thanking them for all that they have done for you and your prospect.

- Call or write to your existing customer to inform them of your success when you win the business. Thank and praise them for all their help in securing this new business. Plus, you can also send or personally deliver to them an appropriate gift or token of your appreciation for them and their staff such as a fruit basket for their staff or an arrangement of flowers for their lobby. This will go a long way toward their agreeing to have another prospect visit their offices in the future.

As I have already stated, Corporate Tours and Product Demonstrations are one of the most exciting and key steps of the sales cycle. However, remember that you are arranging the tour and demonstrations. It is your responsibility to coordinate and control all aspects of the event. The prospect is investing their time and depending on you to have their visit a rewarding and pleasant experience.

Arranging a Corporate Tour and Product Demonstration requires much coordination. However, to land prestigious accounts, this is the type of effort that must be expended. This is especially true if you are trying to take an account away from your competition. You can count on the fact that your competition, as the incumbent vendor, is trying very hard to not lose this account.

Take a boxing match as an example. If you are the challenger and the other person is the champion, which is your best way of making sure you will win the match? Is it by just scoring points or is it by knocking out the champion? It is possible to beat the champion by scoring points, but it is not probable. Why? It is because they are the champion. By scoring points you are only proving that you are just as good as the champion, but not better. So the bouts scored on points will usually be awarded to the champion. However, if you knock out the champion, you have proved that you are better and the bout must be awarded to you!

Selling against an incumbent vendor is no different that a boxing match. In order to unseat the incumbent vendor you usually will not win by just scoring points! You must do all you can to knock them out of the sale! Using the selling techniques presented in this book will give you the knock out punches you will need to be successful.

Expect to do some or all of this extra work in order to land a key prospect. When the value of the sale is substantial or when displacing your competitor and acquiring their key account is of paramount importance, extra work will be necessary.

Should you do all of this extra work for every prospect? Just use your common sense and decide which sales opportunities require what amount of effort to land the sale. If you have determined that a Corporate Tour and Product Demonstrations are necessary, the answer would be yes. Depending upon the prospect, the selling situation and sales cycle, you should utilize any combination of the key elements outlined above that are needed to win the business.

Remember, you are arranging the tour and it is your responsibility to control and coordinate all aspects of the event. By following these techniques and putting forth the extra effort you will dramatically increase your closing percentages.

In summary, by following these techniques and investing in this extra effort, your pay back will be a dramatic

You will increase your closing percentages and you will be *developing yourself into a professional salesperson.*

(Please see the sample Corporate Site Visit Agendas and Thank You Letters at the end of this chapter.)

AGENDA #1

ABC COMPANY, INC.

CORPORATE VISIT

TO

YOUR COMPANY

AGENDA

Time	Event	Location
9:00am	Welcome	Your Company
	Corporate Overview Presentation	Sales and Demonstration Center
9:00 - 10:00am	Demonstration	Sales and DemonstrationCenter
	Note All Specific Products To Be	Demonstrated
10:00 - 10:15am	Tour	Sales and Marketing Offices
		Customer Service, Help Desk
		Sales Support, Technical Support
10:15 - 10:45am	Tour	Operations and Engineering Offices
		Product Development/R&D
		Product Managers
10:45 - 11:00am	Travel	Your Company - Corporate Headquarters
11:00 - 11:30am	Tour	Your Company - Corporate Headquarters
		Executive Offices
11:45 - 1:00pm	Lunch	Restaurant Of Prospect's Choice
1:15pm	Conclusion	Sales and Demonstration Center

AGENDA #2

ABC COMPANY, INC.

CORPORATE VISIT

TO

YOUR COMPANY

AGENDA

Event	Location
Welcome	Your Company
	Sales and Demonstration Center
	Corporate Overview Presentation
Overview	Products - Services - Support
Review	Proposed Solutions And Their Benefits
Demonstration	Sales and Demonstration Center
	Note All Specific Products/Solutions To
	Be Demonstrated
Tour	Sales and Demonstration Center
	Sales and Marketing Offices
	Customer Service, Help Desk
	Sales Support, Technical Support
Tour	Operations and Engineering Offices
	Product Development/R&D
	Product Managers
Travel	Your Company - Corporate Headquarters
Tour	Your Company - Corporate Headquarters
	Executive Offices

AGENDA #3 (With A Site Visit To A Customer's Office)

ABC COMPANY, INC.

CORPORATE VISIT

TO

YOUR COMPANY

AGENDA

Time	Event	Location	Presenter
8:00am	Welcome	Your Company	Yourself & Your Manager
8:00am - 8:15am	Corporate Overview	Sales and Demonstration CenterCorporate Overview Presentation	Marketing Department Manager (Name)
			(Insert Name Of)
8:15am - 9:15am	Tour Of Support Center	Customer Service	Departmental Manager
		Help Desk	Departmental Manager
		Sales Support	Departmental Manager
		Technical Support	Departmental Manager
		Operations	Departmental Manager
		Engineering Offices	Departmental Manager
		Product Development/R&D	Departmental Manager
		Product Management	Departmental Manager
		Marketing Office	Departmental Manager
		Sales Office	Departmental Manager
9:15am - 11:30am	Product Demonstrations	Sales and Demonstration Center Note All Specific Products To Be Demonstrated	
	Yourself And Your Product Specialist Team		

AGENDA #3 (continued)

11:30am - 11:45am	Travel	Your Company Corporate Headquarters	
11:45am - 12:00 Noon	Tour	Your Company Corporate Headquarters Executive Offices	Executive Management
12:00 Noon - 1:00pm	Lunch	Restaurant Name	Yourself and Your Manager Product Specialist Team Executive Management
1:00pm - 1:20pm	Travel	Name of Your Customer Who Has Agreed to Host A Site Visit/Demonstration For Your Prospect	Name of Customer Staff Member Who Will Be Hosting Your Prospect's Visit to Their Site
1:20pm - 2:00pm	Tour	Your Customer's Site	Names of Customer
	Product Demonstrations	Note All Specific Products To Be Demonstrated	Staff Members Who Will Be Conducting Tours And Product Demonstrations
2:00pm	Conclusion		

Date

(Prospect's Name)
(Prospect's Company Name)
Company Address
Company City, State and Zip Code

Dear Prospect:

I just wanted to sincerely thank you for taking so much time to visit with (Your Company's Name) on Friday. I know that you have a very busy schedule and everyone appreciated the opportunity to meet and present to you, Prospect #1 Name and Prospect #2 Name.

We do trust that we were able to give you a high level of confidence in (Your Company's Name), our unique service/support capabilities and guarantees and our robust suite of products and services. We trust that you were satisfied with the total number of our trained and certified technical support personnel, their many years of experience, level of technical knowledge and the depth of our support staff.

We at (Your Company's Name) are looking forward to designing and implementing our proposed solutions at your new office location and working closely with your staff at (Prospect's Name). It was a pleasure having you visit (Your Company's Name) and for giving us the opportunity to showcase our Customer Service and Support Centers and Technology Development Department.

We look forward to servicing your xyz needs and building a long-term relationship with (Prospect's Name).

Regards,

Your Name

Title

(Your Company's Name)

cc: Your Sales Manager's Name and Title

(Your Company's Name)Date
(Prospect's Name)
(Prospect's Company Name)
Company Address
Company City, State and Zip Code

Dear Prospect:

Tom, Mary and I just wanted to express our sincere thanks for giving (Your Company's Name) so much of your time on Thursday to present our product and service solutions for your xyz office.

We were pleased to learn that there were many different features and capabilities of our proposed solutions that met your xyz needs. We do hope that we were able to explain these options clearly and that all information was presented in a straightforward manner.

We do trust that we were able to give you a high level of confidence in (Your Company's Name) and our approach to providing you with a choice of solutions to meet your needs and objectives. (Your Company's Name) technical staff is Factory Trained and Certified. Our technical support personnel also have many years of experience and a high level of technical knowledge on all of the proposed solutions.

It was a pleasure presenting to you. We at (Your Company's Name) are looking forward to designing and installing whichever of the proposed solutions you should choose.

Should you have any questions on any of the subject material, please call me at (Your Telephone Number).

We look forward to servicing your project needs and developing a long-term relationship of serving your xyz office.

Your Name

Title

(Your Company's Name)

cc: Your Sales Manager's Name and Title

(Your Company's Name)

PROPOSAL PREPARATION, STRATEGY AND PRESENTATION

B E PREPARED! YOU SHOULD PREPARE everything you need for your proposals and presentations before they are due. By this I mean you must complete proposals, assemble additional handouts, test all demonstration equipment or assemble props ahead of time. This will give you time to relax, clear your head, review all the materials and remember to complete anything you may have forgotten.

Is this additional work? Does this mean that you have to be organized and disciplined with your time management resources? The answers are yes! You may even surprise yourself regarding items that need to be corrected or topics that need to be changed. By performing these steps, not only will you discipline yourself to review all the material and make whatever adjustments are necessary, but you will also be very prepared and confident when presenting your work.

Proposal Preparation: Benefits Of Taking Extra Time To Prepare A Proposal:

By investing the extra time to properly prepare proposals, you will begin to set yourself apart from inadequately prepared competitors. Some of the important benefits of adequate preparation are as follows:

- Your prospects will notice and appreciate all the preparation work you have done for them.

- Your prospects will see how confidant and well prepared you are just by the way you conduct yourself when presenting.

- They will also respect and have confidence in you for the sincere effort you are putting forth on their behalf.

- You will have the peace of mind knowing that all materials are in order. Because the proposal is complete and presentable, your mind is actually free to concentrate on your customers buying signs and answering their questions.

- You can also concentrate on addressing your prospect's issues and needs, including those that you created earlier in the sales cycle that are of benefit to your prospect.

- You can focus on taking advantage of and even creating opportunities to qualify, seek agreement and trial-close prospects on their important needs and issues.

- You will also close more sales by being well prepared.

- Take the time to make your presentations and proposals easy to read and understand. Structure your proposals to be "self-presentable". This will enable your prospects to review your material later without you having to be present to interpret the information. Many prospects will make their buying decisions from proposals that are clear and self-explanatory.

- Check and re-check all information on proposals and presentations. Do "dry runs" by presenting proposals or presentations to yourself, your peers or manager, family or friends, etc. We all need to practice more before making presentations! Accept critiques openly and in the spirit that someone is trying to help you. Leave your ego at home. Usually you will realize that you needed practice after all.

Proposal Strategy:

A proven technique is to present an account with at least two proposals that contain satisfactory solutions to their needs. If there are two other competitors presenting one solution each, you will have more of an opportunity to be a *consultative sales person*. With this example you are giving an account the opportunity to choose between your Option #1, Option #2, Competitor A's Option #1 and Competitor B's Option #1. In this scenario, you are offering two options to each one of your competitor's options. Your chances to win in this scenario are increased.

By presenting more than one proposed solution, you will generate more discussion and questions about your options.

The account will have more confidence and reliance in you because of the extra effort you are putting forth to provide them with alternative solutions. This technique also gives you more opportunity time in front of the account to hear what is on their mind as they discuss your options. This also avails you additional time to posture yourself as a consultative salesperson. The added benefit is that the more time you are with an account discussing your solutions, the less time they have to spend with your competition.

Proposal Presentation Techniques:

Most companies already have proposal formats developed for presentation to prospects. If permitted, do not hesitate to be creative with different and unique professional approaches to presenting your company's proposals. Keep things simple and easy to understand. You do not want to dazzle them with your brilliance and creativity, but have them miss what it is you are presenting!

The presentation of a proposal should include:

- A documented review of all the system analysis and design work you and your prospects have completed together.

- A reiteration of the needs assessment and related solutions that both you and your prospect have discussed and agreed upon.

- A formalized, documented review of the account's needs, objectives, issues and problems.

- Your documented solutions of how you intend to meet and resolve these items to the accounts satisfaction.

- Your proposed solutions that are grounded by the successful affirmations you have received when trial closing.

- A summary of the advantages and benefits the account will realize from your products, services and support offerings.

- A summary of value added benefits of doing business with your company.

- A list of your customer references, preferably in the prospect's line of business.

- Pricing options along with add/change/delete schedules.

• ORDER FORMS TO APPROVE!

Do not forget to present order forms for the account to review and approve. I strongly recommend you have order forms available for the account to *see* even though you know they will not be giving you an approval. The reason is that this technique gives the account the opportunity to get over the psychological impact of actually *seeing* the order forms for the first time. It also lessens or eliminates the account's emotional trauma when it is time for them to give their final approval on these order forms. Have all the necessary forms available when presenting several different types of purchase or financing options (e.g., purchase, lease, rental, special financing). The account is expecting you to ask for the order and to present the order forms so do not disappoint them!

When presenting a proposal, if you notice a mistake, do not get rattled. If it is not a major mistake, ignore it and just keep right on presenting. If the mistake is major and ethically it must be addressed, simply admit it is your mistake, take full responsibility for the error and explain why or how it most likely occurred. Mistakes may be a typographical error, a financial miscalculation on your part, incorrect information typed or you just plain forgot to include or consider key information, etc. Never blame the mistake on anyone else but yourself and then move on.

If you are presenting a written proposal that has a mistake, a good practice is to immediately take out your pen, correct the mistake and initial the correction. This professionally solidifies the correction, closes the issue and allows you to move on. You should also make a copy of the corrected material for your records and leave the original corrected document you have initialed with your prospect.

If you are making a slide presentation or any type of presentation where you physically cannot correct mistakes immediately, simply note the corrections on tablet paper and initial your corrections. When you are finished with the presentation, make copies as indicated above giving the original documents with corrections to your prospect.

As a professional salesperson, keep your meetings relaxed. Even if you checked your material ahead of time, you will still miss things. Everyone makes mistakes. Do not make a big deal about it. Note the corrections, do not get upset and just keep on presenting.

When presenting a proposal along with order forms to an account at their office, make sure a setting and time of day is chosen that will be comfortable for the account. Present the proposal by going over all details of the order documents with the prospect, particularly where items relate directly back to your proposal. If the prospect begins to read the order forms in more detail, especially terms and conditions documents, be quiet! Give them all the time they need to read the information. Do not speak and break the silence. Let the account be the first one to speak to ask questions, make comments, etc. A final technique is to present the proposal to them at your office! This involves asking them for a commitment and investment of their time. By doing so, this technique can enhance your probability of closing the sale.

CHAPTER FOURTEEN

PRICE CHANGES AND SALES PROMOTIONS

I F LEGITIMATE PRICE CHANGES OR sales promotions occur during the sales cycle, present these to your prospect in an honest and straightforward manner. Immediately present back up documents to verify the accuracy and integrity of the sales promotion time frame as well as when price changes become effective and expire.

Situations such as these will also help you to determine whether or not you have a valid prospect. They may help to speed up a prospect's decision-making process to take advantage of current proposed pricing, especially with prospects that would normally take a long time to make a decision. These situations may also reveal that an account is not a prospect at this time. This does not mean that you are to abandon this prospect. It simply means that you, and they, were able to determine that they were not ready to make a buying decision at this time.

An important concept to realize is which of your accounts are not in a position to buy now regardless if there is price change or sales promotion available. It is best to leave these accounts alone until they are in the final decision making process. To present them with price changes will accomplish nothing. Presenting them with sales promotional pricing too soon in their buying cycle may create regret in their mind now and in the future. They will regret the fact that they are not in a position to take advantage of this pricing now. The account will also remember past promotional pricing opportunities missed in the future when they are ready to buy. They may ask you if the special pricing is still available. If it isn't, there is now regret on the account's part and probable embarrassment for you. Plus, you will now have created a needless objection to buy based on current non-promotional pricing that you must now overcome.

Only present price changes and sales promotional pricing to prospects that are in the final buying stages of their sales cycle or those prospects that you feel are ready to be moved into this final stage.

CHAPTER FIFTEEN

HAVING BREAKFASTS/ LUNCHEONS/DINNERS WITH ACCOUNTS

THERE ARE OCCASIONS DURING A sales campaign when it is appropriate to invite the prospect to meet with you for breakfast, lunch or dinner. This should be viewed as a festive business occasion. By accepting your invitation the account is not only investing additional time with you on a somewhat social basis, they could also be indicating that they are viewing you as their vendor of choice.

This is an excellent time to build not only a strong business relationship with the account, but also a friendly personal relationship as well. These occasions are opportunities for you and your account to be in a relaxed environment. I would like to present some proven guidelines to ensure a successful meeting.

- When scheduling a breakfast, luncheon or dinner with an account, make sure they have agreed to set aside the necessary time.

- Ask the prospect what type of food they prefer and if they have any specific restaurants they would like to visit.

- Choose a convenient location that is close to the accounts office.

- Choose a location that is close enough to all other scheduled events (e.g., visits to your office or customer sites) so you do not fall behind in your schedule.

- If possible, pick the account up at their office and drive them to the restaurant. This will give you additional time to be with your account to build and strengthen your personal relationship with them as well as discuss your proposal.

- If the restaurant's location is unfamiliar to you, drive the route you will take ahead of time. This will save you from the embarrassment of not being able to locate the restaurant.

- Personally visit the restaurant ahead of time and meet with the headwaiter to make your reservation. Explain to them that this is a business meeting and you need their help to select a table that is in a quite area and out of the mainstream of traffic. Upon arriving, if you are running on a tight schedule, also make this known to the headwaiter. For these occasions, headwaiters at the finer restaurants are usually most helpful and delighted to be of assistance. Personally tip the headwaiter for their assistance. Be liberal with your tip! The headwaiter will appreciate your generosity. Whenever you return to their restaurant, you will always be assured of exceptional service.

- When ordering a meal, try to let the account order first. Then order your meal to compliment their selection. You should not order a meal that you will have to wrestle or struggle with. Order a meal that will allow you ample and easy opportunities to converse with your account. Ordering moderately priced meals with moderate portions is always a prudent decision.

CHAPTER SIXTEEN

KEEPING IN CONTACT WITH PROSPECTS DURING A LULL IN THE SALES AND DECISION MAKING CYCLE

So far you have:

- Found your qualified prospect.

- Conducted successful fact-finding appointments with the prospect.

- Identified the prospect's needs.

- Create agreeable new *issues* that favor your company.

- Prepared and presented your proposal.

- Personally taken them on a corporate tour of your offices.

- Possibly even taken your prospect to a customer's office for a site visit.

- Successfully demonstrated and/or presented your products or services to the prospect's satisfaction.

- Qualified and trial-closed your prospect and they are agreeing that your products or services would be of benefit to them.

- Presented the completed order forms to the prospect for their review and approval.

The prospect has been indicating that they feel they can do business with you. However, in order to make a decision, they indicate a need for more time. This may be because they want to consider the competition's products or services. They also may be requesting extra time to consider alternative solutions to their needs or deal with factors that do not involve you or competition. You now realize that your sales cycle, which was moving along smoothly, has suddenly stalled.

What you now have is a lull in the sales and decision-making cycle. What do you do during this lull period? How can you stay in contact with your prospect during this time period without being an annoyance or jeopardizing your opportunity to make the sale? If this lull extends into weeks, months or even longer, what do you do in the meantime?

What you are encountering is just another step in your sales cycle. Of course you will not be pleased to learn that this extra step has developed. However, as a professional salesperson, you have learned to expect the unexpected. With this additional step occurring, you must now be prepared, ready to adapt to this situation and move forward with a positive attitude.

The development of this additional step is also an opportunity for you to demonstrate patience and consideration with your account. You must now be prepared to re-address the steps learned in **Chapter 10: Step 5 Of The Sales Call**. The purpose of this chapter was to **discuss and define what the next steps are to be in the "Sales Cycle."** So once again, you must re-define the following action items with your prospect:

Action items:

- What are you to do next?
- What does your prospect want you to do next?
- What is your customer or prospect to do next?
- Clearly define and assign these action items to each other.
- Establish a time-line.
- Seek Agreement.
- Schedule the next meeting.

By doing this you will be re-establishing a new plan of action and time-line. In essence, another step has been added to your sales cycle! Remember, the customer's decision-making time frame is what is most important.

Ask the prospect what they would like you to do? Normally, the prospect will ask you to call them back in a few days, weeks or months. However, if they say anything similar to they "will call you when they are ready to revisit the project," you must immediately qualify them by saying that if you do not hear from them by a prescribed time, will it be ok to call back to check in with them? The answer should be yes. If the answer is not yes, you may need to ask more questions in order to determine if you are working with a valid prospect.

When checking back with a prospect, make sure that you do so at the agreed upon time. If there is still no decision forthcoming, confirm the next time that you will check back with them. Do not be discouraged if they ask you to call them back again and again. It is better than having them tell you to not check back at all or they have chosen to do business with your competitor.

It is not unusual for these lull scenarios to continue for many months. This is because there can be many circumstances beyond the control of you and your prospect that can easily cause delays. (i.e., unexpected budget issues, sudden high priority critical expenditures, business or economic downturns, etc.)

When lulls occur during a sales cycle, I recommend that you also consider the following additional techniques:

- As long as the prospect is willing to have you to stay in contact with them, you have nothing to lose and everything to gain. Patience, consideration, persistence and professionalism will pay off in the long run. Investing time by staying in contact with a prospect will increase your chances of successfully closing the sale. This will become most apparent after you have won a sale and your new customer informs you of the reasons you prevailed. Some of the reasons may be:

  - Because you stayed in contact with them and followed up at the prescribed times.

  - Gave them enough time to make their decision.

  - Were genuinely interested in being of service to them.

  - Because your competitors lost interest in the sales opportunity.

- Never abandon a prospect unless they instruct you to do so. If the sales campaign begins to be drawn out, always stay positive and professional. The prospect was originally willing to initiate their investigations and meet with you. Perhaps their original plan was just to begin researching products and services to satisfy a present or future need and were not expecting to find a solution with you so quickly. Perhaps, other business and/or economic conditions may be occurring that dictate they change their original plans and the prospect may not want to or be in a position to share these issues with you.

- When you sense the prospect is hesitating to move on to the next logical step of the sale or that the sales cycle is unexpectedly slowing down or actually stopping, simply ask the prospect if they are prepared to move forward or would they like more time to review your information. If they want more time to review information, again just refer to **Chapter 10: Step 5 Of The Sales Call**. If they answer no because they do not want to move forward at all, verify as to what is causing this situation and how and when their circumstances may change.

- As reviewed earlier in this chapter, ask if you can keep in contact and check-in with them in a month or two. Normally a prospect will agree to this approach. If they do not agree, ask them why. Perhaps you or the prospect would prefer to stop investing time in the project.

- If your prospect is open to you keeping in contact, agree to a time frame. Then, every month or so, send them information regarding happenings within your company or any other information you deem appropriate but not pushy. Always attach a personal note to any material you send.

- Also, whenever you see a newspaper article or any publication regarding your prospect, send the information to them along with a personally written congratulatory note.

- Be creative and try different methods and ideas of staying in contact with prospects. Be imaginative and open to the possibilities of new ideas and methods.

So do not be surprised when sales lulls occur. Use them as opportunities to be respectful and considerate of your prospects situation. They will usually appreciate you for your patience and understanding.

CHAPTER SEVENTEEN

REQUESTS FOR INFORMATION (RFI), REQUESTS FOR PROPOSALS (RFP'S) AND REQUESTS FOR QUOTES (RFQ'S):

THESE REQUESTS FROM ACCOUNTS CAN be great learning experiences because when you respond to them, you actually learn much about your company, services, support and products. However, they can also be a very involved, time-consuming and resource intensive process. Depending on how you have received or obtained the RFI, RFP or RFQ, they can take you away from spending valuable time with valid prospects. This chapter will address what to do when you receive an unsolicited or solicited RFI, RFP or RFQ.

An unsolicited RFI, RFP or RFQ is the most suspect type of request. These are the ones that have been prepared by the prospect or maybe even by the competitor and the so-called *opportunity* has arrived completely unexpectedly. You have never called-on these accounts. You have not had an opportunity to *influence* or be involved in the development of the request. Where did the account get the information to prepare their request? How long have they worked to prepare this request? Has a competitor already influenced this request? Why did the account not consult you or your company when preparing their request? Have they already made their vendor choice, but need to solicit multiple bids? Is the request written specifically toward your competitors' products or services? Are you *locked-out* of the opportunity before you even start?

All these questions should run through your mind when receiving these unsolicited requests. They must be answered to your satisfaction. These questions do not mean that you will not have a chance to be competitive, but usually your probability to win under these circumstances may be slim. If the requests are written in such at way that they are very generic, all vendors may have an equal chance of winning.

So you have this unsolicited RFI, RFP or RFQ in your possession. What do you do next? Here are some suggestions.

1. Visit the account and ask the fact-finding and qualify questions as reviewed in **"Selling Essentials" Chapter 7: Qualifying And Fact Finding.**

2. Ask them why they chose to send their request to your company. This is a key question. Make sure you are satisfied with the answer or is the account using you as a *price-check*! We will study *price-checkers* in **"The Secrets Of Selling" Chapter 28: Price-Checkers.**

3. Ask the account who helped them prepare the request. Was it a consultant? Was it one of your competitors?

4. If it was a consultant, is it one with whom you are not familiar? If so, perhaps you may want to meet with them to learn if there are any other evaluation requirements they are willing to consider, especially those requirements that would be beneficial to you. Ask them with which vendors and products are they most familiar? Are they at all familiar with your company? Have they already had positive experiences with your competition? Are they truly open to other vendors?

5. If there is a consultant involved, have you had a positive experience with them in the past? If not, why? Do you have experience with them always awarding business to bidders other than your company? Do you feel they are inviting you to bid because they have to produce several bid responses to satisfy their client and they need a few vendors to *participate* in the response exercise? Based on your past experience with this type of consultant, you can politely excuse yourself from

responding. If they ask why you do not want to participate, tell them the truth. It is better to not waste your valuable time if you have a track record of not winning with a particular consultant.

6.   Do you feel that you can develop a positive relationship with the account or consultant in a short period of time?

7.   Decide how much time and effort it will take you to respond with respect to your other promising prospects. Will working on this request detract from closing your other valid opportunities?

8.   Do you have the time to work on this unsolicited opportunity as a learning experience or are you already busy with valid prospects?

Review all the above information with your support and management team to assess the request material and decide if it is a prudent business decision to participate in the request. Determine if this opportunity is being presented on a level playing field or is it really an opportunity for your competition. If your company does want to respond, make sure your manager puts together a response team and stays involved to manage, direct, energize and motivate this team to help you respond in a professional and timely manner. Do not try to respond to large, complex involved requests by yourself. Again, get your sales manger involved to form a response team. Above all use your common sense and trust your own instincts. If the opportunity does not feel right, it probably is not right!

Over time, experience will prove to you which type of RFI's, RFP's and RFQ's you will have a likelihood of winning.

These will be with the accounts where you have had an opportunity to *fairly influence* and solicit the request. Solicited RFI's, RFP's and RFQ's are the ones that you know are going to be issued ahead of time. These requests will be issued by accounts with which you already have had a positive business relationship and feel that you will have a fair chance of winning the opportunity.

There is still one more type of RFI, RFP or RFQ that you may receive. It is one that you have solicited and have had an opportunity to *influence* or be involved with. However, the request looks nothing like what you expected. It is very general in nature and addresses many important areas either in vague terms or completely ignores them. It puts the burden on you to sort everything out to meet their *undefined* needs and if you do not meet these needs, it is your responsibility to bear the consequence and expense. If this sounds confusing it should. I have experienced these types of requests. I call them the *crystal ball* requests. You will need a *crystal ball* to sort out what is going on and you will never be right or satisfy the account anyway. These are usually immediate losing propositions. They are the type that set up the winning vendor for failure. Do not participate in these requests. Leave these for you competition to work on. It will keep them busy and off the street for long time making it easier for you to work with valid prospects and win business.

Before we leave this chapter, I do want to state that there can still be value in responding to the above types of requests even though you feel you have a low probability of winning. The reason is that these scenarios can actually be opportunities to gain additional experience and learn a great deal of information. As stated earlier in this chapter, you can learn more about your company, services, support and products because you have to articulate this information by responding in writing.

You can also use these particular occasions to:

- Learn your competition's pricing tactics.

- Understand how your competition positions their products and services against your company.

- Experience how your competition positions their strengths and benefits against your company.

- Learn more about your competitors' sales strategies, techniques, marketing positions and tactics so you can plan on how to overcome them in the future.

- Practice how to overcome your competitor's above strategies and marketing positions.

- Better prepare yourself to successfully compete against your competition when you have a valid prospect and have a better probability of winning the opportunity.

In essence, by responding to selected RFI's, RFP's and RFQ's you can learn how your competitors are successfully selling against you. Once you are armed with this knowledge, you will be better prepared to sell and win against your competitors in the future. You will have the knowledge of how to prepare for and counter competitor's sales strategies, techniques and tactics.

Information and knowledge are power! Sometimes, the only way you can gain the competitive information edge is to participate in some sales opportunities you feel you will not win in order to gain much needed competitive power!

I will review this topic in more detail in **Chapter 27: Trust your Instincts and Chapter 28: Price-checkers.**

SELLING ESSENTIALS
PART FOUR:
BUYING SIGNALS, TRIAL CLOSING, CLOSING AND NEGOTIATIONS

CHAPTER EIGHTEEN
BUYING SIGNALS

BUYING SIGNALS CAN BE VERBAL comments or non-verbal body language displayed by the prospect that indicates they are becoming more in-tune with what you are presenting. As time goes on they are giving the outward *appearance* (verbal or non-verbal) of becoming more receptive, agreeable and accepting of the solutions you are presenting. It is important that you recognize when buying signals are being sent. The following are examples of verbal buying signals.

Verbal Buying Signals:

- The account actively and enthusiastically partakes in discussions during the sales call.

- They are more receptive to exploring and openly discussing different options and methods of meeting their needs.

- They will ask questions and make comments that signify they are assuming possession.

- How soon can you deliver your product or service?

- Can you deliver/install the product before the end of this month?

- Can we order the product in different colors or quantities?

- Could we order a partial shipment?

- Can we implement the services you are proposing in phases?

- The product seems to be adequate for our future growth.

- Your proposed solution does seem to be flexible enough to meet our needs.

- When we do this with your company..........

- Can we do this or that with your product..........

- Do you take credit cards?

- Would you consider payments over time?

- What are your payment terms?

- Do you offer special financing options?

- How much of a down payment to you need?

Verbal buying signals are much the same as the statements you make when trial closing, except the account is expressing these statements.

Non-Verbal Buying Signals:

- You receive a genuinely warm welcome when you arrive at their office. You feel as though they gave been sincerely looking forward to your arrival. Your experience and instincts tell you that you are working with a valid prospect.

- Perhaps when you first met with the prospect they instructed you to sit in a chair across from their desk. However, in ensuing meetings, they are *inviting* you to sit in a chair *alongside* their desk or at a meeting table in their office.

- The account has become more courteous and accommodating to you.

- Upon your arrival you are offered something to drink, asked to hang-up your jacket or anything that indicates the account is inviting you to stay.

- You may notice that they seem to be leaning forward and listening a bit more intently to what you are saying.

- They show more enthusiasm and interest in your discussions.

- During meetings, they appear to be nodding their head in approval.

- Scheduled meetings last much longer than planned. Examples are ½ hour, 1 hour or longer.

- The account refuses to take telephone calls or be interrupted while you both are meeting.

There are many types of buying signals. You just need to be alert and observant to realize they are occurring. When meeting with accounts, be relaxed and observant. Be aware of the time and space around you! By doing so, your common sense will reveal when buying signals are occurring. Conversely, if you are not experiencing any buying signals during your sales call, you may not be working with a valid prospect.

In **The Secrets Of Selling, Part Two - Chapter 29** of this book, I briefly review the fascinating topic of **non-verbal body language.** This is a different spectrum of human interaction that is available for you to learn how *listen* to what your prospects are *telling* you by simply *observing* their body language toward you. I do recommend that you read books dedicated to covering this intriguing method we use to communicate with each other.

CHAPTER NINETEEN
TRIAL CLOSING

What Is Trial Closing?

TRIAL CLOSING CAN BE COMPARED to taking your prospect's temperature. You should be taking their temperature in the sense that are they becoming inclined toward you and your company's products and services as their vendor of choice.

With trial closing, you are not trying to close the sale or ask for the order. You should be asking questions during sales calls to determine whether or not the prospects are in agreement with you and what you are presenting. During your consultative sales calls you will be asking qualifying questions to determine a prospect's needs. You will also be analyzing their operations, designing solutions or making an actual sales presentation. During any of these selling scenarios you should be trial closing.

When Should You Trial-close?

Trial-close early and often! Trial-close throughout the entire sales cycle! Trial closing should be blended and woven continually throughout every sales call you conduct. It should become a natural part of your consultative selling process.

Why Should You Trial-close?

You should be trial closing and seeking agreement for five main reasons.

1. To confirm that the prospect is in agreement with what you are presenting and that you can continue on with upcoming steps of your sales cycle.

2. To qualify the account that you are satisfactorily meeting all of their objectives and needs.

3. To validate that your proposed solutions are of benefit to the prospect and resolves their issues and problems.

4. To uncover any hidden objections or issues as soon as possible so they can be addressed and resolved.

5. To logically lead the prospect to the closing step of the selling cycle.

In essence, you do not want to be asking for the order and discover that you have several key issues and objections that are still outstanding or have never been discussed. This is not to say that this will not happen in the real world of selling, but by trial closing early and often, the occurrence of these events can be kept to a minimum.

The following are examples of various types of trial-closing questions.

General Trial Closing Questions:

- Do you see how the benefits of my product or service will enable you to meet your objectives?

- Do you feel that the feature or functionality of my product or service will be of benefit to you?

- Do you agree that the solutions I am presenting to you will be of benefit to you?

- Do you feel confident that our company can service and support your account?

- Are you comfortable with all the information I have presented to you today?

- Do you agree that our products and services will meet your needs?

- Are you satisfied with the cost savings our services will provide to your company?

- Do you agree that we can improve the efficiency of your operations?

- Are you satisfied with how we can increase your level of customer service and support?

Specific Trial Closing Questions:

- Are you confident that my company can provide you with a higher level of service and support than the other vendors?

- Do you agree that our products and services will give you more growth and productivity than other vendor offerings?

- Can you see how implementing my proposed solution will give you a competitive edge over your competitors?

- Are you satisfied with the return on investment our company's products provide compared to other vendor solutions?

- Are you confident with my company's proven track record of delivering excellent customer service and that we will be able to support your account?

- Do you feel that the product we are discussing will give you more initial capacity and long-term growth compared to the other products you have seen thus far?

- Do you feel as though we can do business together?

Notice that you have not asked for an order with any of the above trial-close questions. You are only seeking agreement and concurrence with the prospect. Also make notes in your sales portfolio as to the items being agreed to. By virtue of you making notes, you are validating what the prospect deems as important issues and psychologically you are leading them to the closing step of the sales cycle.

Trial closing is a questioning and verification process to ensure that specific issues are still important to the prospect. Trial closing is seeking agreement to ensure that both you and the prospect are on common ground regarding the solutions you are presenting. You are confirming that these solutions are still meeting their business needs and objectives. The trial closing technique helps you to affirm that your prospect is still willing to consider doing business with you and your company.

Trial closing also enables you learn from a prospect if their original needs remain unchanged, have expanded or have been replaced or influenced by other issues. The goal is for their answers to be yes. If their answers are no, you must determine why. Did their needs change? Are there additional factors present that are influencing or changing their requirements? If so, you must develop a plan of action to address these new criteria to your prospect's satisfaction.

Unfortunately, after you have been successfully qualifying, trial closing and have been receiving agreement throughout the sales cycle, there will be accounts who will unexpectedly not recall and deny ever having made previous commitments to you. Some accounts will even change or bring up entirely new criteria and claim that they have been telling you about these all along! Although these situations happen infrequently, they have happened enough to me that I want you to be aware that they do occur. If you ever encounter this situation with a prospect, it may be best to move on and find a more valid, legitimate prospect.

CHAPTER TWENTY
CLOSING THE SALE - ASKING FOR THE ORDER

Pre-Closing Techniques:

PRE-CLOSING IS A TECHNIQUE THAT you can use to set the stage for the close, which is when you will ask for the order.

This questioning technique is used to psychologically prepare your prospect that you will soon be asking them for the order. This pre-closing technique is much like trial closing. You may even reuse some of your original trial closing questions in this step of the sale. The main purpose of this technique is to use the pre-closing questions as segues to the actual close itself and to uncover any of the account's remaining hidden issues.

Sample Questions To Illustrate Pre-Closing Techniques:

- What color would you prefer?

- Would you prefer the item in red, white or blue?

- How many items would you want?

- Do you need one or two dozen of the items?

- Do you prefer item A, B or C?

- Do you prefer the larger size or medium size item?

- When would be the best time for you to have us deliver the product?

- Would you prefer us to deliver the product tomorrow, next week or in two weeks?

- Would you prefer our services package that includes all of your facilities or just the main office?

- Would you prefer our one, two or three week consulting package?

- Would you like to begin utilizing our consulting services now or next month?

- Our staff needs to work closely with your contractor. When do you expect construction on your new building to begin?

- When do you plan to implement the project/process? To meet that date coupled with our delivery/installation lead-time schedule, we would need to have the product/service orders by a certain date.

Customized Pre-Closing Questions:

You will need to customize pre-closing questions such as these to your own personal product line and type of prospect. The overall concept is that you are asking non-threatening questions in preparation to ask for the order. If you have had positive responses to the questions, you are now ready to move into the closing step of the sales cycle.

If the account balks at these pre-closing questions, then it is not time to close. Hidden issues or objections may have now surfaced and are being verbalized by the prospect. This is actually good because you now know exactly which issues or objections you must overcome before you can attempt to close. At this time you must stop and address each issue and concern they may have. You may have to revisit certain stages of the sales cycle and go through that cycle's respective steps. You may have to go all the way back to the very beginning of the entire sales cycle to revisit specific issues and topics. These delays may take only a few minutes or days, but can extend into months.

Once any additional concerns or objections have been successfully addressed or removed, trial-close as before and move into the closing step of the sales cycle.

Closing Techniques

Closing is the most exciting and satisfying part of the selling process! This is where you can finally ask for the order! Many salespeople do a great job in all the other steps of the selling process, but they are hesitant to ask for the order and close the sale. Your goal is to be a great salesperson and a great closer!

Let's assume you have done a good job of fact finding, realizing customer needs, creating additional sales issues and needs and related these needs and issues to your prospect as benefits. Furthermore, you have attained the prospect's agreement throughout the sales cycle and trial-closed early and often. The next logical step in the sales process is that your prospect is waiting for you to ask for the order. So do not disappoint them. Go ahead and ask for the order!

Asking For The Order:

You can ask for the order in many ways. You can simply ask the account if they are ready to give their verbal approval for you to move forward. Normally you will need to ask the account to sign your order documents. In these cases, do not say **"Are you ready to sign my contract?"** This is an intimidating statement and can make a prospect feel uncomfortable at the very *moment of truth*, the moment they are to sign an agreement.

The following are a few proven professional closing techniques. Make these statements in a normal, calm, comfortable manner. If you are nervous, do not let it show! At this time both you and your prospect should be experiencing a sense of excitement and anticipation. The reason is because this is finally the *moment of truth*! All of the hours, weeks, months or maybe even years of hard work both you and your prospect have invested in this decision have come down to this moment! This is a big moment and you should treat it as such.

Use these statements and questions as suggestions to craft your own personalized closing techniques.

- "Are you ready to OK our work order?"

- "All we need is your OK to start the work."

- "If you are ready for us to get started, all you need to do is OK the order."

- "Are you ready to give us your approval on our Consulting Services form?"

- "All that is needed for us to get started is your approval on our Sales Agreement."

- "Your approval on this order form is all that is needed for us to deliver the product."

- "If you are you ready to approve our order form, we can get started on the project immediately."

- "If you are ready to implement the project, all you have to do is give your authorization on our order form."

- "All that is needed to turn your objectives/plans/dreams into reality is your approval for the Scope Of Work."

- "To insure that we can meet your implementation time frame, we would need your authorization to move forward as soon as possible. Preferably today."

- "In order for us to work closely with your construction manager and meet your building project deadlines, we need your approval for our work order as soon as possible." "Can we obtain your OK today?"

Note: In some instances, all you may need is a verbal approval. If so, use the above closing techniques and just leave out the words order form, sales agreement, etc.

The above closing statements are intended to be smooth transitions, not harsh and intimidating. All you are asking for is their approval. The prospect also knows when you are presenting the order form or sales agreement that these documents are contracts. However, the goal is to present the contract in a non-threatening, relaxed, comfortable, upbeat manner.

After any of these closing statements, professionally present the prospect with the order form and a pen. Hand the order form and pen to them or gently slide them across their desk or meeting table. The next step is to Be Quiet! **Do not utter a sound! Do not speak even one word! Be Quiet for as long as it takes the prospect to approve the order. Why? Because, the first one who speaks has given control of the closing to the other person!**

On many occasions I have personally waited many long minutes until a prospect either *approved the order* or *spoke*. Those seconds or minutes while you are waiting will seem like an eternity! The silence will be deafening! However, you must be patient and wait! The longer you wait the more you increase the probability the account will give you their approval. The prospect will need time to make their final decision. They are weighing the advantages of going with you and your company one last time. This can be a particularly difficult final decision period for the prospect if you are replacing the incumbent vendor who has been servicing the account. Be quiet and respectful. Give them the decision time they need.

As a professional consultative salesperson, your prospect should be ready to *buy* from you! You do not have to *sell* them! Closing the sale should be a natural evolution process of the sales cycle. Asking for the order should be a very logical, straightforward, cheerful, optimistic process.

If the prospect declines to give their approval on the order form, simply ask them why they are not ready to approve the order now? Address these reasons by using the methods we reviewed in the Pre-Closing Techniques section in this chapter. Again, you may have to revisit certain stages of the sales cycle and go through that cycle's respective steps.

However, after you done all of the above and you still cannot close the sale, what do you do next? Make sure you understand exactly why the account is not or cannot giving you the order today. Listen to what they have to say. Ask them if you alleviate the issue or remove the obstacle would they buy? If they say yes, then do what needs to be done to clear the path and, again, ask for the order.

If you are still unable to close the sale, ask for help. In some cases you may be to emotionally or physically drained after having worked with an account for a long period of time. The sales opportunity may need a fresh approach. In these cases, have your Sales Manager and colleagues review all your work thus far. Ask them for their advice, insights and ideas. Finally, have your Sales Manager visit the account with you to help you close the sale.

CHAPTER TWENTY-ONE
NEGOTIATIONS

AFTER ALL THE HARD WORK you and your prospect have invested in this sales cycle, the prospect has agreed you are their vendor of choice and they are ready to buy from you. They now want to negotiate the price, payment terms, conditions or service and support aspects of the sale.

In these cases, try to meet or exceed the prospect's reasonable requests for pricing considerations that are within your control to negotiate. In situations where the prospect's request for special pricing considerations, payment terms are outside of your normal scope of authority, try to meet them half-way with options and solutions that are within your area of decision making authority.

However, if an account is asking for certain terms, conditions or concessions that are not within your power to provide, bring in your higher-level management staff to negotiate and close the sale. Invite the account to your corporate offices for a visit to meet your executive staff to negotiate the terms face to face. Offer to bring your executive staff to their office for negotiations. Come up with whatever creative ideas that are logical, ethical and acceptable by your company. As long as the prospect is talking and working with you and is giving you their valuable time, they are interested in doing business with you. The account is still a prospect and, hopefully, they are spending their time with you and not your competitors.

Keep in mind that just because you have now asked your management team to help with the negotiations, this does not mean that you are almost finished selling. Most times you will now have to start your *inside sales campaign*! This new campaign can involve convincing your management team as to:

- Why this prospect will be a valued, profitable account for your company.

- How and why you have developed your pricing strategy.

- Why you feel it would be advantageous for your company to make certain price concessions or increasing levels of support and service at no extra cost for the prospect.

You should also stay actively involved with your management team during this process. You may even have to lead them through the process, especially if there are special terms and conditions or concession issues that need to be considered or developed. Do not be discouraged if you find that you have to work hard to convince this inside team to do what is necessary to close the sale. The objective is for the sale to be a win-win situation for you, your account and your company.

SELLING ESSENTIALS
PART FIVE:
POST SALE WINS AND LOSSES AND HAVING PATIENCE

CHAPTER TWENTY-TWO
POST SALE - WINS

AS A PROFESSIONAL, ACCEPT YOUR wins with grace, honor and dignity. Upon order signing, sincerely thank the account for their business. Indicate that you are looking forward to establishing a long-term business relationship with them.

Do not demean your competitors. Do not brag or boast to others. Always follow-up after the order is signed by sending a congratulatory note or letter thanking the customer for their business and their trust and confidence in you and your company. (**Please see sample letters at the end of this chapter.**)

Follow-up with your customer after your product or service has been installed or delivered to make sure they are still satisfied. Personally visiting the account is always best. However, many times a follow-up telephone call will also work well.

If possible, try to be present at your customer's site during the first day your products or services are implemented. Your customer and support staff will appreciate your presence.

Your best references will always come from your satisfied customers. Something as simple as following-up will count quite a bit when you later ask your customers if you can use them as a reference for a new prospective account.

As time goes on, if you ever see newspaper articles regarding your customer or their company, send these articles to them along with a congratulatory note. Be creative and always look for positive ways to stay in touch with your customers after the sale.

(Thank You Letter To Your New Customer)

Date
(Customer's Name)
(Customer's Company Name)
Company Address
Company City, State and Zip Code

Dear (Customer's Name):

We at (Your Company's Name) would like to thank you for your recent order of the xyz system. I would like to also personally thank you for your trust and confidence in me and (Your Company's Name).

We at (Your Company's Name) are looking forward to designing and implementing the new xyz system in the upcoming months. We want to assure you that we will do our utmost to insure that the xyz system implementation will progress smoothly and with no disruptions to your current operations.

Again, thank you for your confidence in me and (Your Company's Name). We at (Your Company's Name) are looking forward to building a long-term partnership with (Your Customer's Name).

Sincerely,

Your Name

Title

(Your Company's Name)

cc: Your Sales Manager's Name and Title

(Your Company's Name)

(Thank You Letter To A Consultant)

Date
(Consultant's Name)
(Consultant's Company Name)
Company Address
Company City, State and Zip Code

Dear (Consultant's Name):

I just wanted to thank you for your recommendation to (Customer's Name) to have (Your Company Name) provide them with their new xyz system.

We are looking forward to designing and installing their new system and working with their staff. We are sure that they will be very pleased with their new xyz system and our xyz services for their ancillary needs.

(Consultant's Name), it was a pleasure working with you. We at (Your Company's Name) look forward to working with you and (Consultant's Company Name) on future projects.

Sincerely,

Your Name

Title

(Your Company's Name)

cc: Your Sales Manager's Name and Title

    (Your Company's Name)

CHAPTER TWENTY-THREE
POST SALE - LOSSES

DESPITE ALL OF YOUR BEST efforts, you will experience losses as a sales person. As a professional, you must accept your losses with grace, honor and dignity. Do not demean your competitors even if you are certain that you worked harder and proposed a better solution. Do not complain to others about your loss or misfortune. Loosing a sale does not mean that you are an incompetent salesperson. There can be many reasons beyond your control that you were not aware of as to why you were not favored with a prospect's business.

You must keep a positive mental attitude even in the face of losses, no matter how staggering, because the next prospect you talk to will know nothing of your losses. It takes courage, discipline and determination within your character to move forward after a sales loss. However, as a sales professional, you must move forward with a positive attitude as quickly as possible. You must always present yourself as a confident and enthusiastic salesperson no matter what the prior circumstances have been or what they are now.

You must be upbeat and ready to try again with the next prospect. You may be just the salesperson for whom this next prospect has been searching for to solve their needs. They may be very excited to talk with you and you must be poised, ready and in positive frame of mind to talk with them. Is this easy to do after having just experiencing a loss? Of course not, it is very difficult. However, as a professional salesperson with a strong sense of character, you must discipline and train yourself to go forward no matter how difficult the task. You must develop and adhere to the principles of keeping an outward positive frame of mind and attitude at all times. You will be building your character so that you will have confidence in yourself. You must have the courage and commitment to continue onward in the face of personal or professional adversity. By doing so, only then will you learn that the best remedy for a lost sale is a brand new prospect!

When you lose a sale, request a meeting with the account to review why they choose the other vendor over you. Make notes of these reasons or perceptions. Analyze and review them. Develop ways to identify, address and counter these items for future sales opportunities. You may also discover that the account was never really a prospect for you and your company.

Consider sending a note or letter thanking the prospect for giving you the opportunity to bid for their business. Express your regrets that they did not choose you and your company and ask them to keep you in mind for future opportunities. Emotionally, this is a most painful and difficult task. However, it should be done because you never know what opportunities this account may present to you in the future or who they know in your business community. Although you lost this time, you can still let the account know that they were dealing with a true professional salesperson. They may just give you another sales opportunity or a valid referral in the future. (**Please see sample letters at the end of this chapter.**)

Next, follow-up with this account near the time the proposed product or service is to be delivered as well as afterwards. There is always the possibility that your competition may not be able to deliver or perform up to the level they promised or at a level that is acceptable by the account. The account may be willing to reconsider your proposal. This does happen often enough that follow-up telephone calls to lost accounts maybe worthwhile.

In the sales profession you must prepare yourself to loose sales opportunities. However, the positive aspect of a loss is that you will always learn something to better prepare yourself for the next prospect. Plus, you can always work hard and find other prospects that are willing to consider you as their vendor of choice.

The best analogy regarding lost sales that I have learned is comparing a salesperson to a baseball player. If a ball player's batting average is .300 they are considered a very good player. However, it also means that they either struck out or were unsuccessful in getting on base 7 out of 10 times! They did not achieve their goal 70% of the time, but the 30% of the time they do makes them a very successful ball player! So do not let loosing sales opportunities discourage you. Keep on working hard to develop the sales techniques presented in this book and you will be successful.

Date
(Prospect's Name)
(Prospect's Company Name)
Company Address
Company City, State and Zip Code

Dear (Prospect's Name):

I just wanted to thank you for taking the time to send me your recent letter informing me that (Your Company's Name) was not successful in our bid to be of service to you.

I also would like to thank you and (other Prospect's Names) for giving (Your Company's Name) and myself the opportunity to present our products and service solutions.

I do regret that (Your Company's Name) was not able to serve you at this time. However, please keep us in mind in the future in case your chosen vendor does not work out to your satisfaction.

We are pleased that you were satisfied with our presentations and explanations of our products and services. I would like to ask that you keep (Your Company's Name) in mind when you are networking with other businesses. Our hope is that you could recommend us to them as a professional, local provider of xyz products and services.

Sincerely,

Your Name

Title

(Your Company's Name)

cc: Your Sales Manager's Name and Title

    (Your Company's Name)

Date
(Prospect's Name)
(Prospect's Company Name)
Company Address
Company City, State and Zip Code

Dear (Prospect's Name):

Although (Your Company's Name) is disappointed that we were not fortunate enough to initially win your business, we do understand why we were not chosen. However, (Your Company's Name) does thank you and everyone at (Prospect's Company Name) for giving us the opportunity to participate in your bid.

Should you become dissatisfied with (The Winning Bidder's Name), we would welcome another opportunity to be of service to you.

In the future, if we can ever be of assistance, please call me at (Your Telephone Number).

Sincerely

Your Name

Title

(Your Company's Name)

cc: Your Sales Manager's Name and Title

(Your Company's Name)

CHAPTER TWENTY-FOUR
HAVING PATIENCE

D
O NOT FORCE THE SALES cycle process. Have patience and do not rush the prospect into a decision. Be considerate and give your prospect adequate time for their analysis and decision making process to take place. Your prospect may want to or have to consider other vendors and options even if you are the incumbent vendor and the account is satisfied with your company and proposal. They may want time to analyze other proposals and options. The decision maker may also need to consult with their staff and that will influence the ultimate decision.

Let the account have the time they need to make a decision. Usually it is not prudent to pressure an account into making a decision immediately. Especially when you sense they are not in a position to make a decision. Ask them if you can follow-up with them in the near future. Normally they will agree. Use your common sense. If you think you should follow-up in 1 month, double or triple this time and ask if you can follow-up in 2 or 3 months. This technique will quickly put the account at ease and give them a sense of control. They will also realize that they are not dealing with a high-pressure salesperson. Their response will normally be to agree or even ask you to follow-up sooner than what you suggested, which is a positive buying signal.

If your competitors are pushy or use high-pressure sales or closing tactics in their sales campaigns, they will surely be undermining their own credibility when competing against you. Plus, if they insist on calling the account every 1 or 2 weeks, they will be viewed as a nuisance. Respect your prospects as professional customers. They have already dealt with many vendors before and will not appreciate high-pressure tactics.

After the follow-up time frame has been agreed upon, always remember to ask the account if there is anything else you can do for them. The best-case scenario is when you can receive their commitment that they want you to do something for them before the next meeting.

This can be as simple as:

- Supplying them with more information.

- Sending them revised pricing.

- Doing more research and analysis regarding a specific topic.

- Obtaining permission to meet with different managers to assess their departmental needs.

If the prospect feels as though you are rushing them, especially if they perceive this is for you or your company's personal benefit, you can quickly lose credibility and possibly even the sale. As you develop your sales techniques, you will begin to realize that each sales opportunity is unique and will have its own sales cycle, sequence of events and decision-making time frame.

When the account moves into the final stage of their decision making process, answer any questions they may have promptly. However, at this final stage you want to make sure that you are the *last vendor* to meet with the prospect. Prospects tend to buy from the *last person* who has met or talked with them. This is where relationship selling really pays off. Remember, your prospects will be buying from **you** not your company.

Subsequently, you may learn that one of your competitors has or will be talking or meeting with the account after you. In these cases, you must be creative and find another reason why you must meet or talk with the account. Keep in mind that some of your competitors will also know and be using some of these **secrets of selling**. The goal of this book is for you to know and use more of these **secrets** than your competition. You must be the *last vendor* to meet or talk with the prospect before they make their final buying decision.

SELLING ESSENTIALS
PART SIX:
YOUR CAREER AND YOUR SALES MANAGER

CHAPTER TWENTY-FIVE

WHAT TO DO WHEN THINGS ARE NOT GOING WELL IN YOUR SALES CAREER

L ET ME ASSUME THAT YOU are working for a good company, a supportive Sales Manager and have competitive products and services. Let me also assume that your selling skills are what need to be addressed. Your Sales Manager will be able to assist you. They are the most important resource you have to help you learn the art of becoming a successful salesperson. They are your primary advocate, instructor and mentor. Seek their help, advice, assistance and the use of their talents. They should also have a vested interest in you. Their income usually depends on your being successful!

Above all, strive to not become discouraged. A salesperson's greatest strengths and character traits are a positive attitude, confidence and the will to succeed when facing adversity or trying times. You may be having bad days, weeks, months or even a bad year. However, with the support and help of your Sales Manager, they can help you apply the sales techniques and methods presented in this book.

When things are not going well in your sales career, there can always be positive reasons and opportunities associated with your situation. You may realize that you have to practice more to learn, develop and apply new selling skills and techniques. You may become more determined to work harder to succeed. My personal philosophy is that you do not always have to be the smartest salesperson to be successful. It is the hardest working salesperson, using their common sense, keeping things simple and applying these selling techniques that will develop the necessary confidence in themselves to become a success.

It has always amazed me of how much good can come out of circumstances I initially perceived as negative. If the situation is out of your control, just let it go. Do the best you can with what resources you have. Do the best you can with what you can control and affect. Then, wait to see what develops. More often than not, situations will work out just fine if you just let them take their course and let other experts do their jobs.

There can be business or personal issues that can distract you from your selling focus. If so, try to compartmentalize these distractions. Try to put them out of your mind when you are making your sales calls. There is no practical reason for taking these issues along with you during your sales day. They are just excess baggage. They will still be there at the end of the sales day. Deal with them when you are finished selling.

Always try to keep moving forward. Develop strength and courage in your character. Try to perceive the glass of water as half full and not half empty. I know this is easier said than done, but you must practice and try. Keep working hard at finding new prospects. Plus, there is nothing better to put more bounce in your step than acquiring a brand new prospect that is interested in working with you.

CHAPTER TWENTY-SIX
YOUR SALES MANAGER

YOUR SALES MANAGER IS THE most important person that will help you become a successful salesperson. They should be your primary advocate, instructor and mentor. They are the key person who should want to help you succeed by:

- Helping you develop your overall selling skills, product and pricing knowledge.

- Ensuring that you are properly and adequately trained in your company and industry's product and service offerings.

- Instructing you as to the key benefits, features and advantages of your products or services and how they provide value-added solutions that can help meet or exceed prospect's objectives.

- Helping you to clearly understand how to position and integrate your company's products and services with related benefits, features and advantages into productive, solution oriented sales calls.

- Teaching you how to present your key products or services and which of their advantages can give your prospect a competitive edge in their industry.

- Coaching and helping build your confidence by role-playing through many different selling scenarios while stressing the various steps of the sales call.

- Conducting actual sales calls with you present to observe their selling skills and techniques (e.g., building rapport, asking fact finding questions, qualifying, relating product and service benefits and features to account's needs, overcoming objections, trial closing and closing techniques).

- Having you accompany them on sales calls to their customers (challenging vs. cooperative accounts) so you can learn how to deal with the different types of accounts and personalities.

- Having you discuss, analyze and critique how they conducted their sales call.

- Being present with you when you are conducting your own sales calls and participating when necessary.

- Observing, critiquing and discussing the results of your sales calls.

- Helping you develop sales strategies and sales presentations.

- Helping you to prospect, qualify accounts and close sales.

- Acting as a buffer for you with particularly difficult accounts.

- Acting as a buffer for you between departments within your own company.

- Standing by you through difficult times when selling.

- Helping you to develop your written, verbal and presentation skills.

- Providing you with overall advice, assistance and guidance

The above are just a few of the many duties of a Sales Manager. Your Sales Manager is your one of your most important resources for success. Use them and their talents wisely.

SUMMARY OF CHAPTERS 1 THROUGH 26 – "SELLING ESSENTIALS"

CHAPTERS 1 THROUGH 26 PRESENT a condensed outline of the basic structure of sales calls and essential selling techniques, strategies and scenarios. These chapters were designed to provide you with the most salient aspects of the sales call and sales cycle. These chapters are also intended to give you proven solid selling skills and techniques that are based on **common sense** and **ethics**. The intent is for you to learn to develop, build upon and depend on these skills and techniques for selling success.

These chapters outlined the basic sequence, structure and scenarios of sales cycles. However, sales cycles can take anywhere from a few minutes to days, months or even longer. Also, the sales cycle sequence can change at anytime for any number of reasons that are beyond your control.

The key is to use the fundamental sales cycle steps presented in whatever sequence or time frame is needed to address each individual selling opportunity. Use these steps as a selling framework around which to customize and build your own personalized **art form** of selling for each of your prospects!

By doing so, your goal is to develop a bond of trust and respect between you and your prospects. This will take your professional selling abilities to the next higher level whereby your prospects will view you as a sales consultant. You will be regarded as a sales consultant who is analyzing their needs and sincerely interested in designing a customized sales campaign and the solutions needed to meet their specific objectives.

The end result of the sales cycle is that the logical conclusion for your prospect is to buy from you. You have analyzed their needs. You have presented solutions that benefit them and meet their objectives. You have also qualified and trial-closed the prospect throughout the sales cycle. You have sought agreement and have received affirmative answers on all issues. The prospect has indicated that your solutions will meet their needs and has communicated their willingness to do business with you. The next and logical step is for you to ask for the order. The concept is that the account will be placing their order with you. Note, I did not use the phrase you sold them. The end result is that, as a consultative salesperson, you are still selling, but the account is comfortable in the fact that you are genuinely helping them and that they are buying solutions for their needs from you.

Remember that anything can and will happen at anytime which can help or hinder your sales campaign.

Customer needs and circumstances regarding other business matters may be such that they have to be addressed immediately. These matters can suddenly take precedence over your sales cycle. The end result is that your sales campaign could come to an abrupt, but hopefully temporary, halt. In these cases, you will have to stay in contact with your prospect during these lulls in the sales cycle until they are in a position to again consider your products or services.

Sometimes business matters can work in your favor and your sales cycle can move quickly. You must be prepared to recognize when these changes occur and be ready to move through the sales cycle briskly in order to close the sale quickly.

You must always be prepared and open to the possibilities. As a professional salesperson, you must always realize that anything can happen at anytime. You should work toward training yourself to be observant with your eyes, ears and mind. Notice what is occurring around you on your sales calls. During a sales call, learn to recognize and anticipate what is happening or what may happen next based on interactions with your client. Learn to read body language and recognize buying signals. Be aware of the time and space around you! Use your common sense and trust your instincts.

There will be many different types of personalities to whom you will be selling. Some you may identify with and others will be completely different than your personality. You have to "bridge the gap" with all types of personalities and learn how to adapt immediately, especially, if there are a multitude of different personalities you are presenting to at the same time. Finally, there can also be many disturbances that occur during your sales call. As a professional salesperson, do not let disruptive events and occurrences throw you off-track during a sales call. Seize upon these events as opportunities and use them to your advantage.

The use of these applications and techniques are where you will begin to develop your own personalized *art form* of selling! In your **mind**, take these concepts with you when making your sales calls. Familiarize yourself with them one at a time. Use and practice each one until they become automatic and instinctive. Eventually you will be able to blend them into one cohesive unit. Your goal is to be able to call upon each concept individually or use any of these techniques together or in any random order when needed. **Remember, becoming a successful professional salesperson is all in your mind!**

By applying these techniques, you will begin to develop into a professional salesperson with your own personalized art form of selling!

On this note, let's move on to second part of this book, "**The Secrets of Selling.**"

THE SECRETS OF SELLING

THESE SECRETS ARE USUALLY NOT found in sales training manuals or taught in sales training courses. They are learned after many years of selling with hard-fought wins and losses utilizing many different sales strategies and techniques in many different sales situations with different type of prospects. The use and application of these secrets are how you will begin to develop your own personalized **art form** of selling! By learning and utilizing these secrets, you can develop and hone your selling skills into an art form personalized for yourself and your selling environment. These secrets are how you will learn to become an exceptional salesperson! This is where you will be able to separate yourself from the competition and successfully sell at a much higher level of confidence and professionalism!

CHAPTER TWENTY-SEVEN

TRUST YOUR INSTINCTS
AND INTUITION

TRUST YOUR INSTINCTS. YOU DO not have to be a seasoned salesperson with many years of selling experience to trust your intuition and common sense. Let your mind be free. Learn to listen to your instincts and intuition. If a sales cycle seems to be going well, you will naturally want to keep pursuing the opportunity. This is especially important if you have had success in winning similar opportunities in the past. Also, look back at other similar sales opportunities and remember how these turned out. If you have won or lost these opportunities in the past, you will be training yourself and developing your instincts and common sense as to what is or is not a favorable and potential winning sales opportunity.

Conversely, if a sales cycle seems to not be going well and things are just not falling into place, are you experiencing the following scenarios?

- The account seems to withhold information and you have to drag details out of them.
- You feel like you are giving more information than you are receiving.
- They want to gloss over important information and details or not provide them at all.
- You are not experiencing any buying signals as to why they want to do business with you.

- They are unavailable for meetings.

- You feel you are being rushed to give a price quote.

- You feel uncomfortable with the account, but you just cannot seem to pinpoint your areas of concern.

- Yet, with all of the above occurring, the account still seems to be a bit to genuinely happy to see you or talk with you on the telephone.

This is the type of account I call the *high-five/glad-hander*. They act like everything is great and you are becoming their very best friend, but in reality, you really do not have an opportunity to do business with them. Again, your instincts are telling you that things just do not seem right. Chances are that the account may have their own bona fide ulterior business motives for giving you an audience. The end result may be that they are already planning to give their business to someone else. Unfortunately, these types of accounts may not be adhering to the same ethical standards as you.

When a sales campaign does not seem to be going well and you have lost sales opportunities in the past with similar characteristics, learn to trust and listen to your instincts and intuition. They will help you to avoid many useless sales campaigns. Move on to another sales opportunity. We will also cover more examples of these potential time wasting early warning signs in **Chapter 28: Price-checkers.**

However, before we leave this topic, there can still be some value to the above type of accounts and sales scenarios. Even if your instincts are telling you that you have a low probability of winning, you may purposely still want to pursue a few of these opportunities. This is because these types of accounts can actually be a chance for you to learn a great deal of information. You can use these particular accounts and occasions to:

- Gain additional experience practicing new sales presentation and selling techniques.

- Learn more about your competition's pricing tactics.

- Understand how your competition positions their products and services against your offerings.

- Experience how your competition positions their strengths and benefits against your company.

- Learn how your competition presents what they perceive to be your company, product or service weaknesses.

- Learn more about your competitors' sales strategies, techniques, marketing tactics and positions so you can plan on how to overcome them in the future.

- Practice how to overcome your competitor's above strategies and marketing positions.

- Experience objections the account presents so as to understand how to overcome them for future prospects.

- Ask the account why they feel more comfortable in buying from your competition.

- Better prepare yourself to successfully compete against your competition when you have a valid prospect and have a better probability of winning the opportunity.

- Learn, analyze and experience the *high-fiver/glad-hander* type of accounts so you can avoid them in the future.

Sure ways to learn these invaluable competitive lessons is by participating in a sales cycle with these types of accounts and obtain as much information about your competition as possible. As an added bonus, the above types of accounts are good arenas for you to practice some of your new sales techniques or presentations. After all, you have nothing to lose and the practice will fine-tune you for the next valid prospect.

Finally, you can learn much from the *high-fiver/glad-hander* accounts by asking the following questions:

- What are the competitor's ongoing post-sale service and support guarantees?

- Why does the account feel that the competitions' products or services are superior?

- Specifically, what are the features or services the account is most impressed with or needs?

- What particular post-sales services or support do they feel exceed your company's offerings?

- Are the competitions pricing or terms and conditions more attractive than yours?

- What types of sales presentations or demonstrations is your competitor presenting?

- Which of your services, product features or benefits are most or least impressive to the account?

- Which of the competition's services, product features or benefits are most or least impressive to them?

- How is the competition countering your products' features and benefits?

- What sales strategy are they using to counter your offerings?

- Exactly why does the account feel that the competition's offerings are superior to yours?

- Does the prospect feel the competition's reputation or financial performance is better than others?

By obtaining answers to these questions, you will learn how your competitors are successfully selling against you. Once you are armed with this knowledge, you will be able to prepare for and counter competitor's sales strategies, techniques and tactics. This will enable you to be better prepared to sell and win against your competitors in the future. Your goal will be to strive to meet with future accounts before your competitors so you can use this competitive knowledge to set the stage and format of the sales cycle to benefit you and your company's products and services.

Information and knowledge are power! Sometimes, the only way you can gain the competitive information edge is to participate in some sales opportunities you feel you will not win in order to gain much needed competitive power!

CHAPTER TWENTY-EIGHT
PRICE-CHECKERS

THESE ARE PROSPECTS WHO HAVE most likely already made up their mind as to the product or service they want and from whom they want to buy. These folks will seem to come to you as a lead from out of nowhere. This is what can be called a real "bluebird" type of prospect. They most likely will arrive as a telephone call. This *price-checker* will be exceptionally cordial and seemingly very interested in you, your company and your product or services. These people are almost too cordial. They will want to meet with you almost immediately. They will be willing to talk with you for longer than normal lengths of time. They will readily have all the answers to your questions you learned to ask in "**Selling Essentials**" **Chapter 7: Qualifying And Fact Finding**. This prospect will seem just too good to be true, but beware; this may not be a prospect at all. They may be a *price-checker!*

Does the conversation seem to be going just a little too good? Especially since this is the first time you have ever spoken with this person. Do they have to many answers to your technical questions just a little to readily available? If you probe deeper and ask even more detailed questions, do they also have these answers readily available? Can they answer questions that you know they should not have answer to unless they have been speaking to someone else first? Are they voluntarily giving you what seem to be abnormal details as to their needs? Does your intuition tell you that the prospect does not seem genuine and that something is amiss? Chances are you are correct.

To continue, if the whole conversation and sales encounter just seems to be as if the prospect is always giving you continuous buying signals, you may very well be talking to a *price-checker*. These types of accounts are the biggest time wasters and confidence busters that you will ever encounter. They can lead you down a path of complete sales cycle frustration and then they buy from their original intended vendor. Afterwards, you will spend a lot of time soul-searching and trying to figure out what you did wrong and second-guessing yourself and start to lose confidence in your abilities. However, in reality, you never really had a valid prospect. You were dealing with a *price-checker*.

Another example is the account that you have been trying to call on and make contact with for quite some time. You may have even sent them your very best introductory material on your company and products. However, they refuse to see you and will not take your telephone calls. They will not even take the time to tell you to go away! Then one day you receive an RFI, RFP or RFQ from them with a very short turnaround time frame. This should definitely set-off all of your *price-checker* alarms. This is classic *price-checking*. This account has usually already made their decision as to their vendor of choice. They just need a few competitive quotes to justify their decision.

The analogy of hiking can be used to define the point I am trying to make. When learning to hike, one of the first things a hiker is always taught is to rely on their compass. It will always be true and point north. When you are being trained as a professional salesperson, always trust your internal ethical compass. Trust your intuition and your common sense. If something does not seem right, it usually is not right. Even if you just cannot quite identify exactly what is wrong or what is triggering your subconscious alarm systems, you can be sure something is usually amiss. Trust your internal ethical compass. These words of wisdom should also be applied to life itself.

In my opinion, I firmly believe that a person's subconscious figures things out very quickly because it is not being bombarded with distractions and interruptions that we have to deal with consciously. Distractions at work such as telephones ringing, interruptions, aggravations, customer problems, office politics and domestic issues all interfere with our conscious state. There is just too much "noise" occurring in our conscious state of mind. It is no wonder why people say they just cannot seem to get anything done anymore. In the corporate world, we are all faced with "having to do so much more with so much less!"

However, in my opinion, our subconscious is not distracted with all of these outside disturbances. It filters out all the "noise" to analyze and determine the status of situations very quickly and has all the correct answers for our conscious self readily available. It just takes time for our conscious-self to "catch-up" to our subconscious-self, who patiently waits for our conscious self to arrive with whom to provide the correct information. It is during this "catch-up" time that I feel our intuition and instincts are our subconscious talking to us. They are trying to give us correct and accurate advice consciously as to what does or does not make sense. So if you cannot quite determine what feels wrong, but you know something is not quite right, just release, listen to and trust your intuition. It is your subconscious trying to give you the correct answers.

Additional Signs That Indicate You Are Dealing With A Price-Checker:

When dealing with a "*price-checker*" either on the telephone, via email or in person, be aware of the following "*price-checker*" signals:

- They ask for or require an abnormally fast turn around time for you to provide a price quote.

- They will not grant you an appointment to meet with them in person.

- They do not want to meet with you to see your product. All they want is brochures and pricing quickly.

- They will decline invitations to visit your corporate offices.

- They decline invitations to view product demonstrations or your technical support centers.

- They decline invitations to visit your nearby customer sites.

- Yet, they keep calling with more detailed questions, want answers quickly and continue to request fast turn around times for requested revised price quotes.

- They gloss over or you detect mild or feigned interest in your product's features or benefits that would normally be critical solutions to their needs.

- They may accidentally "slip-in" a negative comment about your product or company that is uncalled for and out of context with the conversation. Should this even occur during an initial telephone call from the account, it is a very bad sign! They are not intending to do business with you. They just need to *price-check* the vendor they have already chosen.

- They become argumentative and/or confrontational with you and your ideas or solutions. Again, if this occurs during an initial telephone call from the account, you have to seriously question if their intentions are honorable.

- They quote objections given to them by your competitor about your company, products or services. They appear to believe unfair, unjust or incorrect statements made by competition about your company as genuine information. When you try to professionally refute them and reasonably explain the true situation, the account becomes defensive and combative. They become irritated and do not want you to continue your explanations. They indicate they believe that what the competition has told them is true and they are irritated that your explanations now seem to be besmirching the competition! In this example, the account is not a prospect. If the competition is the incumbent vendor for the account, you definitely do not have a prospect.

- They do not have an open mind to what you are presenting and are unwilling to consider the possibilities presented by another vendor's point of view.

- They ask why you are not proposing a product or service that you have never even mentioned. Coincidentally, this product or service would put you at a competitive disadvantage. This indicates that your competitor is prompting them, which is the vendor they have already chosen.

- When you offer valid product or service ideas that will provide them with competitive advantages, the account disagrees with you or discounts your ideas as not important or relative. You present ideas that would even give your prospect a competitive edge in their line of business, but they are disinterested. They are not willing to explore possibilities.

- You begin to think, why am I dealing with this person?

- Your common sense begins to ask you why these encounters with this prospect are becoming increasingly difficult, unpleasant and painful?

- Towards the end of the sales cycle the prospect becomes increasingly difficult to reach. They will not meet with you. They do not answer their telephone. They do not return your voice or email messages for days on end. Then suddenly they call you with a few more questions and requests for revised price quotes that do not play toward your corporate product or service advantages.

- Eventually you will get a curt telephone call or email that says they have already decided on a vendor, signed their contract and they will thank you for all your time and effort. You will feel rather foolish and embarrassed. It will be as if someone has slammed a door in your face. Which, in reality, is exactly what has happened. You have been *price-checked!*

Do some of these examples seem outrageous to you? I can assure you that I have personally experienced each and every one of the above examples. I found these events very outrageous and hard to believe when they occurred to me. However, they are real and they do occur to sales people every day. Be on the lookout for situations and do everything you can to avoid dealing with these types of prospects.

Additional Information Regarding Price-Checkers:

You may be asking yourself why I am spending extra time reviewing this topic of *price-checkers?* Why am I advising you to be aware of these types of accounts? There are four basic reasons.

1. Not every account may want to change vendors or do business with your company for many reasons that are out of your control.

2. The second reason is that there are prospects that will purposely provide you with information that is not totally accurate. They will indicate that they are willing to consider a change or are not pleased with their current vendor, when in reality, they are not displeased or planning to change vendors. They just need to receive a few quotations from other vendors to perform a *price-check* on their current vendor with whom they are quite satisfied.

3. The third reason is that your prospect's company may have a policy that they must receive competitive price quotes on all major purchases even if they are not planning to make a vendor change.

4. The final reason is that *price-checkers* are time wasters and time is a salesperson's most valued asset.

This is why I want to present the following as additional information regarding *price-checkers*:

As I had stated at the beginning of this chapter, this prospect will seem just "too good to be true." The time frame they are giving you to produce a price quotation seems to be abnormally short. Things begin to just not feel right. Things just do not seem to add up. The prospect seems to be just a bit to enthusiastic, pushy or eager to have you invest your time, your most valued asset, in them. Trust your intuition. The reality of the situation or opportunity is that things are not as true as they seem and that you may not be dealing with a prospect at all. This prospect is your "*price-checker*."

The above signals are significant. When you begin to detect these *price-checker* signals, how can you professionally assess the situation? How can you determine if you are dealing with a valid prospect or a *price-checker*?

Reference, **"Selling Essentials" Chapter 7: Qualifying And Fact Finding - Questions #1 through #5, and #21 through #26.** You must receive satisfactory answers to these questions! Even if you do, you must still keep bringing these answers up and use them as qualifying and trial-closing tools throughout every step of the sales cycle. By doing so, especially if and when you have opportunities to meet with other members of your prospect's management team, you will eventually ascertain whether or not everyone shares the same desire to change vendors.

There will be occasions when you will be in meetings with a prospective account where new and different members of their management team are in attendance with whom you haven't met with as of yet. Meetings such as these are golden opportunities to professionally qualify and trail close everyone regarding why you are there and the benefits of doing business with your company. You should also seek agreement that everyone present shares the same desire and conviction to change vendors as does the original staff members you have been working with. If everyone present agrees that they are willing to do business with you, then keep selling. If everyone present does not agree or some hesitate, especially the new members of their team, you may be in a *price-checking* situation.

I learned this the hard way by forgetting to trial-close on just this point presented above. I had an account where I was trying to displace my competitor who was the incumbent vendor. I assumed I had been receiving truthful information from the original staff I had initially been meeting with when they assured me that they wanted to make a change in vendors. However, this was not the case at all with them or their upper management. When the upper management was present for the first time in a subsequent meeting, I failed to qualify and trial-close them on their interest and intentions in changing vendors! Had I done so, I would have immediately learned that upper management had no interest in changing vendors! Had I trial-closed upper management when the opportunity presented itself, I would have also quickly learned that the original staff were not being forthright with me and were just *price-checking*.

So, when new personnel begin to show up in a competitive account during a sales cycle, make sure to qualify and trial-close them on just what you are there to do for them. Do not be shocked if everyone in the account does not share the same convictions. Ask those present that disagree with changing vendors as to why they feel this way? It best to know who these folks are and why they feel this way. This will enable you to determine if you have an opportunity to influence them as to the benefits of why they should choose your company. If you are experiencing difficulty accomplishing this task with a number of the key management staff, you have to determine whether or not you are working with a valid prospect.

Excusing Yourself From Price-checking Sales Scenarios:

As a sales cycle unfolds, the desire to change vendors may not be shared by everyone in an account. If this is the case, you must decide:

- Is it worthwhile to spend one-on-one time with the dissenters to change their viewpoints?

- Do you still have a realistic opportunity to displace the incumbent vendor?

- Should you minimize the time you have already spent on the account and excuse yourself from the opportunity in a straightforward and professional manner.

You can also use the direct approach if your business experience and instincts still tell you things are not right. With this approach you may risk insulting the prospect or *price-checker*, but most times you will get to the heart of the issue quickly. Professionally and sincerely ask this type of question: "Overall, it appears that you really may be satisfied with your current vendor/supplier and would just like to receive a few comparison price quotes? Is this the case?"

A true prospect that is being honest, ethical and has nothing to hide from you will readily disagree and will normally not be insulted. The account will react to this question in the same way they have calmly reacted to all of your other qualifying questions. All you have done is ask a question in a professional and respectful manner and the account has answered appropriately.

An account that is *price-checking* will usually act highly insulted that you would even ask such a question and they will let you know. They will vehemently disagree with you. Their overreaction to the question is usually because they do have something to hide. They may act insulted, but only because you asked a reasonable question in a professional and respectful manner and have exposed their ulterior motives.

In these cases you can congratulate yourself for you have just uncovered a *price-checker*. You have just saved a lot of your valuable time and energy by not getting caught up in the realm of *price-checkers*. Because a *price-checker* is not a valid prospect, you will usually have little or no chance of winning their business. However, you may decide to still provide a price quote to professionally represent your company, but you will know to expend as little time as possible with this account.

Keep in mind that *price-checkers* can be very good at *price-checking*. They may have years of experience and very accomplished *price-checking* skills. However, now that you are aware of the secrets of *price-checkers*, you also have the professional selling skills and insights to be more confident in determining the validity of your prospects.

Advantages Of Purposely Working With Price-Checkers:

Before leaving this topic, I do want to point out that there can be advantages of purposely working with *price-checkers*. In **Chapter 27: Trust Your Instincts,** I recommend that you not spend a lot of time on the *high-fiver/glad-hander* type of accounts. However, you may still want to continue pursuing them because you want to use these particular selling opportunities to gain experience and knowledge. The same is true with *price-checkers*. With these types of accounts, as well as those referenced in Chapter 2, you can **practice** new sales approaches, product demonstrations and presentations. You can also **practice** different trial closing techniques, methods of overcoming objections, pricing options, competitive analysis presentations, etc.

When you realize your prospect is a *price-checker* you do not have to immediately abandon the opportunity. It just means that you are now to proceed with caution. The *price-checker* accounts can be turned into valuable opportunities for self-training and learning experiences. Besides, other than a prudent investment in time, you have nothing to lose and might have everything to gain. I can personally attest to the fact that I have developed some of my best sales presentations, strategies and competitive analysis work while dealing with prospects where I already knew I had little chance of winning. You can use these types of accounts as trial runs to *practice* and refine your selling skills and techniques. The benefit is that when you have your next group of valid accounts you will also have your next level of selling and presentation skills polished and ready to be put to work to land more valid business.

When dealing with accounts that you have determined are *price-checkers*, remember that as a professional salesperson **time** is one of your most valuable assets. Use it wisely.

CHAPTER TWENTY-NINE
NON-VERBAL BODY LANGUAGE

NON-VERBAL BODY LANGUAGE IS A very interesting and intriguing method that we use to communicate with each other. You just have to listen with your eyes and your mind! By doing so the person you are dealing with will be telling you just how the meeting is progressing!

Understanding non-verbal body language will enable you to interpret a wealth of information being provided to you by people. By being able to decipher non-verbal body language, you will be able to obtain answers to many of the following sample questions when dealing with accounts:

- How is the account interacting with you?
- How were you greeted by the account? Were they genuinely happy to see you?
- Where did they suggest you should sit when you entered their office or the conference room?
- Did they suggest you sit in a more favored location the second time you met with them?
- Do you understand the dynamics of how seating subconsciously occurs or is strategically arranged at a conference room table?

- Do you know how to effectively arrange your support staff at a conference room table or in a meeting so as to provide maximum benefit to you and your presentation?

- Based on the dynamics of a prospect's staff, do you need to strategically position your support staff in the audience so they can help you maintain control of a presentation?

- Is your prospect attentive and interacting with you during the sales call?

- Are they interested in what you are presenting?

- Are they maintaining eye contact with you?

- When presenting to accounts, can you tell if they appear "open" or "closed" to what you are presenting? If the account is originally "closed" to you, can you distinguish when they are becoming more "open" to you?

- Do their body actions and demeanor suggest they are willing to do business with you?

- How is the prospect's staff interacting with you? Are staff personnel taking non-verbal cue from the key person?

- When you meet with a prospect's staff for the first time, can you pick-out the key decision maker?

- Do they appear to want to meet with you again?

I recommend that you read books on non-verbal body language. These books contain a wealth of information you can apply in all types of business and personal settings. Once you learn how to recognize and interpret this method of communication, a new and different spectrum of human interaction will be available for you to *listen* what people are *telling you*. By *listening* to their non-verbal body language, they will be *telling you* the status of your rapport with them and exactly how your sales calls are progressing.

CHAPTER THIRTY

Interruptions Are Your Friends, Keep The Sales Process SIMPLE, Think BIG

Interruptions Are Your Friends:

DO NOT BECOME DISTURBED OR frazzled when interruptions occur during a sales call. Welcome interruptions! Interruptions are your friends! Use the extra time that they provide you wisely. Interruptions are opportunities that provide you with time to:

- Take a break during the sales call and gather your thoughts.
- Examine what you have been presenting or discussing.
- Review the account's reaction so far. Are they positive or negative?
- Determine if you have to make any adjustments to the meeting.
- Determine if you have forgotten to review any important topics.
- Review key needs or buying motives expressed by the account.
- Plan on how to weave these key issues into the remainder of your sales meeting.

The more patient you are when interruptions occur during a meeting, the more appreciative the account will be of your professionalism. Stay composed and continue your meeting after each interruption. The more patient you appear, the more you will endear yourself to your prospect. They will realize you are not easily distracted and are calmly giving them the time they need to handle other critical matters.

Keep The Sales Process SIMPLE:

You must strive to keep the selling process SIMPLE. Keep the sales process easy to understand and straightforward.

It is important to always be creative, but stay away from using gimmicks. Avoid structuring a complex sales process because you will most likely confuse the prospect as well as yourself. Do not use your industry's acronyms or speak in complex terms that are too technical or foreign to the prospect. You will probably only impress yourself and confuse the prospect. If you have confused a prospect, it is unlikely they will buy from you. If issues, products or services by their nature are complex, you must strive to present them in simple, straightforward terms in which your prospect can understand. Use analogies they can relate to in their line of business. Draw simple pictures or diagrams they will recognize and comprehend.

If your prospect understands your explanations and product advantages better than your competition's, they will be more comfortable buying from you. They will also appreciate the extra effort and time you are taking to help them understand what you are presenting.

Think BIG:

Do not hesitate to look for and pursue large sales opportunities. They will entail additional time and work. However, they can be an easier sale to work and win versus small sales opportunities because your larger prospect is usually more knowledgeable in what they want and need. Although the sales cycle for larger opportunities is usually longer, these accounts can get right to the point as to what they require. Plus, if you calculate all the time you would need to spend for many smaller sales to equal one larger sale, you almost always will have spent less cumulative time on the larger sale.

I am not advocating that you not work on the smaller sales opportunities. Smaller accounts are valuable sales opportunities. They are your bread and butter prospects that can refer you to larger accounts. I am advocating you work on selected small and large accounts at the same time. Sales to smaller accounts will pay your bills. Sales to larger accounts will help you to put money in the bank.

Think Big! Someone has to win the big deals. It might just as well be you!

CHAPTER THIRTY-ONE

RELATIONSHIP SELLING AND CONSULTATIVE SELLING

Developing Mentors And Dressing For Success

Relationship Selling:

ESTABLISH PERSONAL BUSINESS RELATIONSHIPS WITH each of your accounts and prospects. People buy from people. They will buy from someone whom they like, trust, have confidence in and respect their character. They will buy from professional sales consultants that have taken the time to understand their objectives and are helping them meet their needs. Always keep in mind that your accounts will be buying from you not your company.

The following are ten important fundamental rules to follow when employing relationship selling techniques.

1. Be caring, considerate and respectful of your prospect at all times.

2. Learn your prospect's personal interests and hobbies. Become familiar with them and, when appropriate, broach them as a topic of conversation during your sales call. Pay particular attention to the special occasions when your prospect will be participating in these areas of personal interest. You must be sincerely interested when discussing these topics with your prospect. Insincerity will be quickly detected by your prospect.

3. If possible and appropriate, learn about your prospects family members, their names, and areas of interest. Be genuinely interested about any important events occurring in their lives.

4. Learn the prospect's business and understand:

   • Their business operations.

   • Their physical plant by asking for a tour of their facilities.

   • Why they have certain business functions in place.

   • Where specific improvements are needed.

   • How they intend to implement these improvements.

   • How these improvements will be of benefit to them.

   • When they intend to finalize their vendor choice.

   • Who are the decision makers and recommenders?

   • Who will be influencing their decision?

5. Work diligently to meet and satisfy each of your prospective account's needs. Strive to always be the first vendor to respond and provide the prospect with the information they need.

6. Qualify and trial-close after you have met each of their needs.

7. Always provide the extra effort and be creative to please your prospect. They will recognize that you are trying hard to win their business and will appreciate your efforts and tenacity on their behalf.

8. Always try your best to meet or exceed your prospect's expectations. The prospect will realize, recognize and respect your efforts.

9. Always follow-up in a timely manner regarding all issues and projects.

10. Adhere to the highest of ethical conduct and moral standards at all times. In doing so your accounts will appreciate and respect the fact that your character is impeccable. Your goal in relationship selling is to be viewed as a consultant to your prospects and accounts. They need to understand and embrace the concept that your intent is to develop a genuine, long-term relationship and partnership with them.

Consultative Selling:

Position yourself as a Sales Consultant. Let's analyze the term *sales consultant*. When meeting with a prospect for the first time, you should be in a *consultative* role. You need to fact find, understand what your prospect is trying to accomplish, analyze their short term and long term needs and goals, then design, price and present proper solutions. However, if you cannot meet your prospect's needs and objectives, you must be honest with your prospect and yourself. Tell them that you cannot meet their needs and determine if this is a sales opportunity that should not be pursued. Please review **Chapter 7: Step 2 Of The Sales Call -Qualifying And Fact Finding – Additional Important Questions.**

Next, you are to advise and guide your prospect in determining which solution will best meet their needs and objectives. Yes, this is where the *selling* takes place, but it is in a mode where the prospect respects you and is appreciative of all the consultative and analytical work you have been doing for them. The end result is that the prospect is in a mode where they trust you. They will *buy* from you more so than you have *sold* them. This is what consultative selling is all about. Your main objective is to build mutual trust and respect and help your prospect accomplish their goals rather then just selling them products or services.

Developing Mentors:

Work with successful salespeople in your company. Look for a seasoned salesperson to be your mentor. Ask them what they are doing that is making them so successful. Ask permission to go out on sales calls with them to observe, listen and learn how they conduct themselves in front of a customer. Observe how they professionally present themselves, your company and your company's products or services. Listen as they honestly answer customer questions, handle objections or create issues. Learn how they structure sales calls and plan to control sales cycles.

Ask them how they decide what they will be trying to accomplish and how they develop their strategy before a sales call. Learn what strategy they use to position themselves and your company as the supplier of choice. Discuss the outcome of sales calls with them. Ask them how they handle the *high-five/glad-hander* and *price-checker* type of accounts.

Next, ask to actively participate in your mentor's sales call by asking questions, fact finding or even presenting part of their presentations or proposals to their account. This technique works especially well when your mentor explains to the account that you are learning and that they are helping you to gain some experience. In these instances, customers will usually be very cooperative and helpful. They will also think highly of your mentor for taking the time to help you gain experience.

Having a mentor is not meant to replace your Sales Manager. It just gives you the opportunity to learn from another successful salesperson. With a mentor you now will have an additional person with whom you can learn the finer points of selling techniques for your industry. Some of these finer points are as follows:

- How do they find their prospects?
- Whom do they meet with when calling on a new account?
- What are their successful selling strategies?
- How do they analyze an account's needs?
- How do they develop and present their pricing and proposals?
- How do they overcome and answer objections?
- How do they successfully sell against competition?
- How do they manage their time and stay organized?
- Do they demonstrate your products?
- Do they take prospects to visit their existing customers?

Dressing For Success:

You only have one chance to make a good first impression! Your personal appearance should always be as professional as possible. You should be well groomed and dressed appropriately for your climate and clientele.

We all know of the saying, "you should never judge a book by it's cover." However, in personal and business relationships, there is no way around being judged. You will be judged and treated by other people based on the way you behave and dress. Whether we like it or not, that all important first impression judgment will be based on your *cover* and how you present yourself to people.

Dress appropriately each day based on the types of accounts you will be calling on. Wear appropriate clothing if you will be at manufacturing site and around a shop floor production area all day. The same applies if you will be visiting a construction job site or a recreational site. Conversely, if you will be at formal meeting settings in offices or making presentations to prospects in conference rooms, you should now choose attire that befits the occasion.

You may also be calling on accounts on the same day that are at opposite ends of the clientele spectrum. If so, consider bringing along extra attire that allows you to *dress-down* and then *dress-up* for each respective sales call. If you are ever in doubt as to how to dress for a specific occasion, err on the side of *dressing-up* with clothing that will enable you to *dress-down* to suit the event.

There can be occasions when you may be calling on an account that you know will be having a special type of corporate event. If the event is such that your normal business attire would be out of place, just get in with the swing of things!

I once had to make a sales call to a prospect's office to pick up a sales agreement. I was informed that everyone was going to be dressed in Halloween costumes all day. I knew that my normal business attire would be woefully out of place. What do you suspect I did? You guessed it! I made the sales call dressed-up in a Halloween costume! Everyone in the office had a great time and was appreciative that I made the extra effort to *blend-in* and join in their event. The sales call went very well. The account approved the order and we are still doing business to this day.

The purpose of this story is to encourage you to be flexible and adaptable when selling. "Think outside of the box." Be creative and let your mind be "open to the possibilities." Be daring. It takes courage and confidence to do so, but the personal rewards can be great. Read books on dressing for success. They contain a wealth of information.

CHAPTER THIRTY-TWO

WHAT TO DO WHEN PROBLEMS ARISE IN YOUR ACCOUNT AFTER THE SALE

What To Do When You Lose Your Key Contact In An Account
Competitive Considerations

What To Do When Problems Arise In Your Account After The Sale:

POST SALE PROBLEMS WILL INEVITABLY arise with accounts. When problems develop, do not shy away from them. Problems are actually opportunities for you to prove just how professional salespeople and their companies step forward to fairly and equitably resolve issues. Work diligently with your accounts to identify, address and creatively resolve the issues. Even if other support personnel are responsible for resolving the issues, I recommend you stay visible and connected with the resolution process because if things are not working out to the accounts satisfaction, you are ready and present to intervene with other suggestions.

Accounts will always be appreciative when everyone on your team steps forward quickly to address issues. By doing so, your accounts will realize that you and your company are showing respect and a sense of urgency for their concerns. This relieves their anxiety and they will be more ready and agreeable to resolve issues in a spirit of teamwork and cooperation.

After issues are resolved, I also recommend that you verify and affirm with your account that they are now satisfied with the resolution. No matter how great the problem, as long as you and your company are visible and actively involved in the resolution process, accounts will always be appreciative of everyone's efforts.

Even if your company has to absorb costs to rectify problems, the time and money spent will be an inexpensive investment towards ensuring and protecting excellent customer relations. It will always cost your company more money to obtain a new customer than to retain an existing customer! Customer goodwill and loyalty are invaluable assets toward building a good base of customer references and obtaining future sales referrals.

When things are going smoothly in an account, account management is easy for everyone. However, when problems arise, it is the true sales professionals that do not shy away from, but step forward to resolve issues. Always make certain that your existing accounts are loyal and satisfied. They are the lifeblood of your company.

What To Do When You Lose Your Key Contact In An Account:

Loosing a key contact in an account when they leave for another job or are reassigned in their company can be a very disappointing event. This can be especially frustrating when you have invested time with that person, have developed a rapport with them and they were preparing to buy from you. However, as a professional, you are now prepared for the unexpected and must be ready to move forward.

The first thing you must do is to stay in contact with the account. Know what their plans and time frame to replace this key position. After the replacement person is hired, be the first vendor meet with them to introduce yourself and your company. Explain that you were working closely with their predecessor and are looking forward to working with them. I recommend that you do not attempt to launch into a full-scale sales campaign at this juncture. Just explain to them that you are very familiar with their operations and have been analyzing their issues, needs and objectives as outlined by their predecessor. Offer that you would like to review with them your work and conclusions thus far, whenever they may be ready to do so. At such time, you would also be interested to know if they have come upon any new issues that need to be addressed.

Do not be high pressure with this new person. Be considerate of the fact that they are new and will need time to get acclimated to their position. However, you do want to be available to be the first vendor to be working with them when they are ready to move forward from where their predecessor left off.

You must be prepared to reinvest the original time and effort spent all over again with the new person. However, do not let this be a sense of frustration to you. Your goal is that this situation will be a sense of frustration for your competitors! Your objective is that they will be unwilling to invest the necessary time to rekindle the sales opportunity. If so, they will be at a definite disadvantage when competing against the sales professional who is willing to put forth the extra effort. This extra effort will also be recognized by the new contact. They will appreciate the fact that you are truly concerned and trying to be of help to them and their company.

Keep in mind that it takes time and effort to find new prospects. You already have time invested in this company. If they are still a qualified valid prospect, it will behoove you to nurture this new person and start a new sales campaign with them. All it takes is patience and your willingness to make the extra effort to start over. In this scenario, you do not have to find a new qualified prospect. You already have one. It is just that your original sales campaign has had an unexpected development. You should be able to spend less time cultivating this account to get them back into a decision making mode versus having to find a new prospect.

Competitive Considerations:

Your primary goal must be to have a complete knowledge of your products and services. You must always be an expert on your product line. However, you must also know as much as you can about your competition. Although you are selling your products and services and not the competitions, you must still be familiar with their strengths and weaknesses. You will ultimately succeed in selling by stressing your advantages over the competition's disadvantages, but refrain from referring directly to your competition by name. When necessary, you must also learn how to turn your product or service weaknesses into strengths.

Use the fact-to-face selling time you have in front of your prospect wisely. Your prospect will want to hear all about your company's products, services, advantages, why they should do business with you and how you can meet their needs. Do not discuss your competition during a sales call. The prospect will have ample time to meet with your competition and hear what they have to say.

Try to know all that you can about your competition (company, current financial status, products, services, strengths, weaknesses, pricing tactics and selling strategies), but never demean or criticize them. If your prospects ask you about your competition, give them the information they request professionally. Your prospect may ask or comment about your competition's business problems, lack of ability to be competitive or even say that they do not like your competition or their proposal. In these instances, always be compassionate and professional with your responses.

Do not agree with your prospect regarding their negative comments about competitors. They may be trying to test the strength and principles of your character by giving you an opportunity to speak in a disparaging manner toward your competitors. If you do so, you will have just lost credibility in their eyes. Prospects who are very experienced buyers will have many ways to test the integrity of the person with whom they are dealing.

A good technique to disarm a prospect in this mode is to actually complement your competitors. You may offer a comment such as your "competitor is a fine company with good products and services. However, many of our customers have chosen our company because they have felt our company offerings were more advantageous for their needs." A statement such as this is not only disarming, but it is a professional lead-in to get the sales call back on the positive track to discuss your solutions.

CHAPTER THIRTY-THREE

REVEALING THE 120 FUNDAMENTAL SECRETS OF PROFESSIONAL SALESPEOPLE

IN ADDITION TO ALWAYS REMEMBERING your prospect's name and title, try to apply the following secrets of professional selling until they become an automatic part of your normal selling process.

1. Be ethical and honest in all matters. Your accounts will recognize and value this important character trait in you.

2. Sustain and protect your integrity and honor at all times. Accounts will want to work with sales consultants who maintain the highest of moral standards. By doing so, accounts will not hesitate to refer you and your company to their business associates.

3. Be true to yourself and your character at all times. This will enable you to have faith and confidence in yourself and give you the strength and courage to pursue and attain your goals.

4. By upholding your ideals and principles to the highest of standards, you can depend on your character and forthright reputation to always precede you.

5.   Ensure that your word is your bond! Many accounts do not need to seal a business transaction in writing. A handshake or verbal agreement is all they will need to do business with you.

6.   Your accounts will value the above character traits in you. They will come to depend on you and respect your advice and professional recommendations. Develop, foster and practice these exemplary and honorable character traits at all times.

7.   How do you define a person's "character"? My favorite definition of "character" is as follows: **"Character" is who you are and what you do when no one is watching!**

8.   Always respect yourself and demand respect from others.

9.   Always show respect to your accounts and competitors.

10.   Always treat everyone with dignity, fairness, respect, kindness, consideration and compassion at all times.

11.   A salesperson's two most valuable assets are their **mind** and their **time**. Your **mind** and **time management** are the key resources to your success.

12.   Continually advance your mind. Always be in a learning mode. Be open to new ideas. Strive to learn more about the selling profession and time management by reading books, attending seminars, joining professional sales related organizations and working with other successful sales people. Keep abreast of the new product and service offerings of your industry. You must always continue to learn and develop new selling talents and skills.

13.   Time management: Protect your time. Use your time wisely. Be organized and disciplined with your time management resources. Do your paperwork at home, not during prime selling time. Plan out your workweek on Sunday evening. Plan out your workday the night before you to go to work. Gas up your car on your way home from work. Try to get all the necessary but bothersome tasks completed so that they do not interfere with prime selling time.

14.   When driving to meet with accounts, arrange your schedule such that you leave home early and travel to the farthest account first and then work your way back home or to the office. If you run short of time and are not able to meet with all the accounts as planned, at least the ones you still need to see are not far away.

15. An organized salesperson is a successful salesperson! Keep accurate, up-to-date customer files. When accounts call to discuss issues with you, it will become readily apparent to them that you have their files at your fingertips. This instills customer confidence in you.

16. Always use a person's name when speaking with them. The most pleasant sound anyone can hear is the sound of their own name. This technique also shows respect and is essential in developing rapport and a relationship with someone.

17. Keep a positive mental attitude and frame of mind at all times. Do not become easily discouraged. Be persistent, but in a professional manner.

18. Make your own "luck." Luck is when preparation meets opportunity!

19. Avoid trying to compete or "measure-up" to other salespeople. Set your own personal goals and do your utmost to attain them.

20. Always strive to do your best. It is better to lose a sale knowing that you have done your best versus knowing that you did not try hard enough to win.

21. View all situations as positive learning experiences, including lost sales.

22. "Be open to the possibilities and think outside of the box." Be daring, creative and resourceful!

23. Have perseverance in your selling campaigns. Be persistent, diligent, determined, disciplined and tenacious.

24. Be patient. Do not rush the sales process. Your prospect will select a vendor based on their own timetable and sequence of events that makes sense to them. You must pace your efforts to be in sync with their goals and time frames.

25. Whenever possible, try to present the account with at least two of your solutions to their needs. This technique will increase your chances of being the chosen vendor (**Please reference Chapter 13.**)

26. Do not be afraid to try and fail. It is better to try and fail than never to have tried at all. The way will you succeed and learn to do things correctly is by first doing them incorrectly. If you are not making mistakes, then you are not learning. There are benefits to failing depending on how you approach a failure or a lost sale in your mind.

Approach failures as beneficial learning opportunities that teach you how not to do things in the future. Lessons learned from failing are usually not forgotten.

27. Whenever possible, try to control the sale and the sales cycle.

28. Qualify, Trial-Close and Seek Agreement early and often!

29. Learn how to recognize potentially good or bad sales opportunities by qualifying your prospect early.

30. Create the customer needs and issues, tie them into customer benefits and seek agreement.

31. Always present your significant competitive advantages up front to prospects. Strive to qualify and trial-close your prospects on these advantages. This is to verify early in the sales cycle that they need the exclusive benefits your products and services will provide.

32. Learn how to take what your prospect presents as a competitor's advantage over your company's product or service and turn it into a disadvantage for the competition. Seasoned competitors will also take their disadvantages and present them to the prospects as advantages. In these cases, you must patiently and professionally explain why this is really a disadvantage to them while presenting the competitive advantages and strengths of your product or service. Other times, competitors will present incomplete information to your prospect and then posture this information so that the prospect perceives this information as advantageous. You must take the same approach as presented above and be careful at all times to not denigrate the competition.

33. Exude confidence and believe in yourself even when you are unsure of the next sales step. You will have time to decide on the next step and your support team should be there to offer advice.

34. Never underestimate your prospect's intelligence. They usually will understand what you are saying and, all things being equal, will judge for themselves if they want to do business with you. Never talk down to them, especially when answering a question or handling an objection. They will know immediately that you are diminishing them and when this happens your sales campaign is usually finished. Present proposals that are "self-presentable". They should be easy to read and understand so that your prospect can have confidence that they can review and compare your proposal to the competition's

proposal. Many sales can be won because the prospect understands your proposal better than the competition's proposal. You will greatly enhance your ability to win sales if there is no question or confusion in the prospect's mind as to what you are proposing with related costs.

35. If your competitor is the incumbent vendor and you are trying to displace them, never underestimate their tenacity and resilience. Even when your prospect indicates they are dissatisfied with the incumbent competitor, do not think you have the upper hand. Keep pressing and working hard to earn the account's business. You can depend on your competitors to fight hard to the very end to not lose their account.

36. When you are the incumbent vendor, always presume there is competition and do your best when presenting your products and services. In today's competitive marketplace, even your most loyal customers will usually be soliciting competitive bids. They are doing this not because they are dissatisfied with your or your company. It is because they either want to do some *price-checking* or because management has instructed your main contact to perform due diligence and solicit a few competitive bids.

37. When you are the incumbent vendor, never assume a competitor cannot displace you. They will be working just as hard to displace you as you have worked to displace them in their accounts.

38. Remember, it will always cost your company more to obtain a new customer than to retain an existing customer.

39. Make sure the prospect is comparing "apples-to-apples" when comparing competitive proposals to your proposal.

40. Keep the selling process SIMPLE. Do not try to impress your prospect by using acronyms, complicated terminology, analogies or explanations. Explain your concepts, products and services in simple, down to earth language that the prospect can relate to and understand. Use analogies that relate to the prospect and their business.

41. Be polite and respectful no matter how much your professional sales call is deteriorating in front of the prospect or how unprofessional the prospect may be treating you. You must have strength of character at all times.

42. When presentations or demonstrations go awry, do not panic, get upset or feel embarrassed. Treat the circumstance in a light hearted manner and even laugh at yourself and the situation. Customers are usually very empathetic and will give you the time you need to pull things back together. Make light-hearted comments to your customer such as: "I've worked 4 hours on preparing this demonstration for you and I'm still making mistakes" or "I've proof-read this presentation 3 times and I still missed this typographical error!" If you have taken the proper amount of time to prepare and have control of the subject matter, you can usually recover in a short period of time. If you are demonstrating a product, you can use such occurrences as opportunities to show your prospect how easy it is to recover from an operational error. In demonstrations, you can even announce to your customer that you are going to make an error on purpose and then show them how easy it is to recover.

43. Stay focused. Work hard on staying focused and on task even when distractions are whirling around you. Break a task down into segments in order to concentrate during the chaos. Whenever you are working on a specific project, whether it be reading mail, administrative duties or developing a proposal, finish it to it is fullest before moving on to the next project. Do not start new projects without first finishing the one you have started. A good rule is that once you start something, finish it so you do not have to go back to it and try and remember where you left off.

44. Be prepared for your sales call. Before leaving your office, make sure that you have everything you will need. When you arrive at the account, take a few minutes to relax in your car or wherever you can find a quite area before announcing your arrival. Use this time to collect yourself and your thoughts. Review your strategy, goals and objectives so that you can conduct the sales call as successfully and professionally as possible.

45. Arrive early for appointments. Here are just a few reasons why: If you get lost enroute, you can still arrive on time. You will not be rushed or harried when you arrive. You will have time to organize and review your material one more time. If you have to deal with inclement weather, you will have time to compose yourself.

46. Expect the unexpected. Always be prepared for the unexpected. The unexpected can and will happen at the most inopportune time!

When the unexpected occurs, be ready to think on your feet, adapt and quickly develop creative and flexible ideas of how to maintain control of the selling situation.

47. Be prepared for disturbances to occur during sales calls. Examples are telephone calls, jack hammers pounding outside, telephones ringing, noisy paging systems, sirens blaring, fire engines or ambulances screaming by, dogs barking, manufacturing operations drowning out your voice, etc. These are just a few true examples of the types of disturbances that have occurred to me while conducting sales calls. Do not get flustered. Maintain your composure and sense of humor to put the account at ease. By doing so, you will endear yourself to the account and save them from embarrassment.

48. While conducting a sales call, if there are any questions or topics for which you do not have answers, place an impromptu call back to your office for help from your support staff. By doing so, you will receive the answers you need and the prospect will realize that your support staff is readily available. Also, for further effect, make the call on a speakerphone so the prospect can hear both sides of the conversation and even join in if they wish.

49. When sales calls involve your having to meet with a number of people in an account, make sure to bring along a team of additional people from your company for support. You do not want a situation where you are the only one meeting with or presenting to many people. Your team can assist you, and also be additional eyes and ears to observe and listen to interactions. Afterwards, you and your team can review the events that occurred during the meeting and be able to accurately plan and formulate the sales strategy for the next meeting.

50. Also, my recommendation is that you should have at least a 2 to 1 ratio of prospects to your staff. So if your prospect is planning to have 6 or 8 of their staff in attendance there should be at least 3 or 4 of your support staff accompanying you to the meeting.

51. Win or lose, always thank and show appreciation to all members of your support team who are helping you to sell.

52. Smile when you are talking on the telephone. The person you are talking to will *hear you smile*.

53. Inform key accounts and prospects of your vacation plans ahead of time. Many times this will spark a prospect into action because they will not want to lose time based on their schedule with you being unavailable.

54. When appropriate, give your important customers and most promising prospects your home telephone number. Especially when working on very important projects that span weekends or holidays. This gives them the opportunity to contact you and proves to them that you are doing your very best to be of service. Accounts will rarely abuse this privilege.

55. Obtain reference letters and letters of appreciation from your customers that you can show to your prospects. Do not hesitate to provide your customers with sample draft letters that they can customize and then give to you.

56. After meeting with your prospect's departmental managers, send letters thanking them for the time they have spent with you.

57. What if you have an account or promising prospect that likes your company and product, but does not particularly like you? Get your Sales Manager involved with the account or even have them take over the account to act as a buffer for you.

58. At times you may be working with accounts that can be difficult or emotionally and physically draining. In these cases, enlist your Sales Manager's help and objective guidance. Another solution can be to turn the account over to your Sales Manager or swap the account with another salesperson. There is no practical reason for you to keep working on an account where there is no chemistry between you both.

59. In addition to your Sales Manager, utilize all other corporate staff resources available to help you sell.

60. Tout and document your company's honors and successes and not your competition's shortcomings. If the topic of your competition comes up during the sales call, treat them with respect even if their valid shortcomings are brought-up by your prospect. As a sales professional, you can lose the respect of your prospect if you choose to *bash* your competition. Defaming your competition will not enhance your ability to close a sale.

61. Stop complaining! Do not allow internal company, departmental or personal issues carry over into your sales calls. There is no practical reason for any negatives to be brought into the sales process. They will greatly reduce your chances of conducting a successful sales call. As a sales professional, you must overcome your emotions and set aside issues and problems when making your sales calls. You may just be the salesperson whom they have been searching for to solve their needs. You do not want to be bringing any negative baggage along with you on the sales call. The account certainly does not want to hear about your problems. They want you to solve their problems.

62. You will be judged and treated by other people based on the way you behave and dress! You will only have one chance to make a good first impression! Your personal appearance should be as professional and impeccable as possible at all times. Read books on dressing for success.

63. Recognize and understand *customer-buying signals*. By realizing when buying signals are being sent, you will be able to interpret this fascinating method of how accounts are communicating with you. Buying signals can be verbal comments or non-verbal body language displayed by the prospect that indicates they are becoming more in-tune with what you are presenting. They represent the outward appearance (verbal or non-verbal) that the account is becoming more receptive, agreeable and accepting of the solutions you are presenting.

64. Read books on "non-verbal body language." Make sure these books have many illustrations to depict their suggestions. These books will teach you about this intriguing method people use to communicate with each other

65. Read books on human relations skills and interaction techniques.

66. If you are not pleased with your presentation skills, take courses on public speaking.

67. People Skills: Always smile and say thank you! Always be genuinely polite, courteous, positive, enthusiastic and gracious.

68. If a valid prospect is late for your appointment at their office, how long should you wait for them to arrive? If you do not have any other following or pressing appointments, my experience has proved that you wait as long as it takes! Specifically, you do not wait just 15

minutes, ½ hour, etc. past the designated time and then leave. You wait as long as it takes the prospect to arrive at their office. Why? The longer you wait, the more you have just increased you chances of winning the sale because you are paying respect to your prospect with your perseverance. When they finally arrive, do not embarrass them because of their tardiness. You can tell them the reason you waited is because you know they are very busy and you did not want to miss an opportunity to have this important meeting with them. This is not meant to insinuate that your time is not valuable. The most valuable thing to a salesperson is their time. However, the account's tardiness is an opportunity to endear yourself to them and can actually be the beginning of your developing a "relationship" with the prospect.

69. Develop a mentor. Locate a person in your company or sales force that has a track record of success. Talk with them. Develop a relationship with them. Ask them questions as to how and why they are successful. You will learn much by commiserating with them. You may even ask them if they would be willing to formally or informally mentor you. Having a mentor is not meant to replace your Sales Manager. It just gives you the opportunity to learn from another successful salesperson. With a mentor you now have someone with whom you can learn the finer points of selling techniques for your industry.

70. *Screeners* or *Gatekeeper* are those people who stand between you and the decision maker in an account. Usually *screeners* are receptionists and administrative assistants. If you are having a particularly difficult time getting past a screener, try visiting the account ½ hour before they open or after they normally close. The *screeners* are usually not on duty at these times. Also try visiting the account around mid-morning on Saturdays. You will be pleased as to how many decision makers you will find still on the job during these non-standard business hours.

71. If you are going to be late for an appointment, call the account and inform them as to when you expect to arrive. Most times they will tell you to take your time. This will take the pressure off you and lower your level of anxiety.

72. Practice your new sales techniques or presentations on accounts that have a low visibility or impact on your selling success. Practicing

with these accounts will give you experience and an opportunity to fine-tune your selling skills and new materials to be presented. In addition, accounts where you feel you have a low probability of winning are excellent accounts with which to present new sales presentations and selling techniques.

73. Always be ready to change and adapt your thinking and selling techniques to current economic or technological developments. Be open-minded. Welcome and embrace change. As the saying goes, "The only thing certain in life is change!"

74. Total Cost Of Ownership: Use Return On Investment or Total Cost Of Ownership financial models. These models will depict the costs for your prospect to operate, maintain, support, upgrade or expand their operations by utilizing your products or services. Your company may also have "value added" customer benefits such as ongoing service and support plans that are superior to those of your competition. Many companies provide these "value added" benefits at no charge to their customers.

75. When delivering or mailing information to prospects such as brochures or corporate introductory information, I recommend you hand write a personal note on your corporate note paper versus typewritten notes. This could be as simple as a thank you note or even a brief summary of what you are providing them with. This is the personal touch that many accounts will appreciate. The purpose of this gesture is to begin to develop your personal relationship with them. Remember, the customer will be buying from you not your company.

76. Deliver information to your prospects *in person* whenever possible. This is because these instances are opportunities to meet and sell to your prospect. When delivering information in person, your presence will usually prompt your prospect to remember additional questions or issues they want to discuss. It also gives you an opportunity to reiterate a few of the most important reasons the prospect should choose you and your company when they are ready to buy.

77. When delivering or mailing information to prospects, always put the selected material into a corporate folder that has inside pockets and a place for your business card.

78. Each time you visit a customer or prospect, make sure to "leave behind" information in large folders that will be hard to misplace or lose.

79. When mailing information to prospects, use big, bulky envelopes that are larger than the 8 ½ inch x 11 inches in size! These are the kind of envelopes that cannot be missed when they arrive! They usually will not get lost in the shuffle of all the other information arriving by mail. Consider using envelopes that are not white in color.

80. Consider hand addressing mailing envelopes to accounts. Again, the personal touch!

81. Be professional when sending letters to accounts. Present the facts accurately and succinctly, but in a friendly and personal tone. Again, you are developing a personal relationship with the account. Also, consider taking courses in professional business letter writing or have your Sales Manager help you to develop your writing skills.

82. Develop your own pre-designed templates of information for use in sales presentations and proposal generation. These templates must be easy to customize for individual accounts. The end result is that you can quickly produce and present professional and customized sales information and proposals for your accounts. You will be pleased at how fast you will build up a sales resource library of information that can be used over and over again for new sales opportunities. Techniques such as this will help you to develop your selling abilities into your own personalized **art form** of selling.

83. When the account moves into the final stage of their decision making process, you want to make sure that you are the last vendor to meet with the prospect. Prospects tend to buy from the last *person* who has met or talked with them. If you thought you were last, but your competitor has managed to meet with account again, you must be creative and develop a reason why you must meet with the account again! This is where relationship selling really pays off. Remember, your prospects will be buying from *you* not your company.

84. Never discuss politics or religion on sales calls.

85. Never discuss social issues that may be in poor taste or are not proper in the context of a professional business environment.

86. Never make offensive jokes, comments or partake in such discussions on sales calls.

87. Be careful when being humorous with accounts. Do not get caught-up in the lighthearted spirit of the moment and say or do something in bad taste that you will regret.

88. Be cautious with an account that appears to be overly joking and cavalier during the sales call. They may just be testing you to determine your character.

89. Prospects may also *test* your level of professionalism and ethics. During a sales call, some prospects will even say and do things that may seem to be unprofessional. However, never go along with them on such things while conducting your sales call. Why? You may feel that, since they are acting this way you should do the same as a method of attaining rapport with your prospect? The reasons are twofold. First, just because they are conducting themselves in an unprofessional manner does not give you license to feed into the situation. Secondly, the prospect may just be testing you! Yes, they will test you! They will be probing to determine if, when given the opportunity, you will compromise your principles and professionalism in order to try and make a sale. If you do so, you may have already lost the sales campaign in the early stages. So always conduct yourself in the most professional, respectable and ethical manner at all times.

90. Follow your instincts and common sense. They are usually right! If something seems wrong, it usually is wrong! If a situation seems strange and something is amiss, it usually is! Let your mind be free and trust what your subconscious is telling you. Perhaps your intuition may be telling you that it is best to move on to your next sales opportunity.

91. Be a good listener. The best conversationalists are always the best listeners. A sales professional that can keep quiet and "listen to the silence" while a prospect is thinking will always be successful. Everyone likes to hear themselves talk. When you are working with a prospect and asking them questions, just listen. Give them time to think. Do not interrupt them. When they pause to think, do not fill the silence with needless chatter. Just be patient and quiet. Give the prospect time to collect their thoughts and express themselves. Also, if you listen carefully, a prospect will tell you exactly what their objectives are and what you need to do to sell them.

92. When meeting with an account, take notes on all the important topics and issues. This will build the account's confidence in you because they will realize you are taking the time to document their needs.

93. Prospects are also professionals. Although you may be a professional salesperson, do not forget that your prospects are also professional prospects. Prospects are also very observant of salespeople. Over the years your prospect will probably have met with hundreds of different salespeople. They will have experienced many types of sales presentations, approaches and personalities.

94. Never underestimate your prospect's knowledge or business savvy. Prospects can be very experienced and professional buyers. These types of prospects will have many ways of purposely testing the integrity of the person with whom they are dealing.

95. Do not be pushy or use high-pressure sales or closing tactics in your sales campaigns.

96. Conduct sales calls from the top down and as wide as possible. Always call as high up in an organization as possible to introduce yourself and your company's products and services. The person you see will be the one who will instruct you as to who the other key personnel are that you should meet within the company. Therefore, as you widen the scope of personnel you are meeting with, you will now be able to let them know that the top-level manager recommended that you meet with them.

97. Interruptions are your friends! Welcome them when they occur and wisely use the extra time that they provide! Examples of these interruptions are when people interrupt your meeting or key personnel temporarily leave and later return.

98. *Price-Checker* type of accounts can be used to *practice* and *refine* new selling skills and techniques. Use them and your time wisely.

99. Try to work on all sizes and types of sales opportunities (small, medium, large). By doing so you will continue to keep your selling techniques and instincts honed and in touch with all the nuances necessary to successfully relate to and sell into all sizes and types of businesses.

100. When problems arise in your accounts, address them immediately and be involved in their satisfactory resolution.

101. Always try to meet and exceed your prospect's expectations.

102. When bringing audio visual presentation equipment out to a prospect's site, always make sure you bring along all necessary back-up components in case of equipment failure. Equipment will fail at the worst possible time!

103. Whenever you see newspaper or magazine articles about a customer or prospect, always send it to them. I also recommend enclosing a personal hand written note congratulating them and saying that you thought they might like to have an extra copy of the article. Send the article in an oversized envelope so as to increase your chances they will not miss the article when it arrives.

104. If you will be visiting one of your accounts to meet with other staff members other than your main contact, always notify this contact that you will be at their site. This will save you the embarrassment of meeting them in a hallway and trying to stumble through an explanation as to why you are there.

105. When meeting with a prospect in their conference room, do not put your attaché case on the conference room table to access your sales or presentation material. Instead, put your attaché case on a chair or on the floor. If you should forget and put your attaché on their table, carefully pick it up with both hands and lift it off the table. Your prospect will notice exactly what you are doing. Account's usually do not like "skid marks" on their expensive, polished conference room tables and will notice and appreciate your concern!

106. Ask for a tour of your prospect's facilities so you can better understand their business operations. Many of your competitors will not take the time to ask for a tour of a prospect's operation. The account will be pleased of your interest in wanting to take the time to learn more about their operations.

107. *Flashes* of brilliance can occur to you at any time. These *flashes* are the solutions to problems or issues, creative ideas regarding a sales campaign or remembering a key comment made to you by a prospect that you now realize is very important. Sometimes multiple *flashes* will occur simultaneously. These *inspirations* and *creative ideas* occur quickly and will not last long. Do not depend on your memory to recall them later on. You need to write them down quickly. They will normally occur when you are relaxed and your conscious mind

is taking a mental break. However, your subconscious has still been hard at work and has been developing solutions to issues. It is not until your conscious mind is relaxed that the subconscious can communicate with you! So I recommend you keep a notepad and pencil handy while driving in your car, relaxing in your easy chair at home and even at your bed stand.

108. When presenting a proposal along with order forms, chose a setting and time of day that will be relaxed for the prospect. If possible, try to present the proposal to them at your office! This technique will enhance your probability of closing the sale.

109. Work with consultants in your industry with whom you and your company have had positive experiences.

110. Be aware of time and space around you. Be cognizant of the big picture.

111. Be consciously aware of "senior citizens" who are "gatekeepers" at reception desks. Many times these folks are key personnel who will or will not permit you access to your prospect. They can be related to management personnel or have been on duty since the company started business. Thus, they actually run and control all office procedures.

112. Don't hesitate to canvass for new business on bad weather days (i.e.: rain or snow). Especially when you have a list of targeted new accounts that you want to visit. The reason for this technique is you can almost be sure your competitors are not out canvassing on these days.

113. In your canvassing portfolio always have customer reference/user lists prepared showing your accounts. Also, if you are responsible for different line of businesses, have specific reference lists prepared for these accounts. Plus, referral letters from satisfied competitive replacement accounts should always be part of your portfolio.

114. Start an email campaign with a small list of targeted prospects along with individual messages written to each prospect.

115. Know your target market prospects and when communicating with them be as personal as possible.

116. Set-up an on-line mini Internet sales presentation (webinar/lunch & learn) to include targeted prospective accounts. Accounts will not even have to leave their offices to participate.

117. Use press releases, company related articles or social media to keep yourself and your company in front of prospects as well as existing accounts.

118. Be prepared to manage your own internal corporate personnel to ensure your sales effort is brought to a successful conclusion. Also, be sure to be on the account's site with your support staff for the implementation of your product or service.

119. Make sure that your support staff always knows that you respect them and are very appreciative for all the support and expert help they provide you on a daily basis.

120. Have a predefined, written set of questions developed to review with prospects to determine whether or not they are a valid prospect.

SUMMARY

I N SOME WAYS YOU CAN liken selling to a puzzle that has to be put together. The puzzle is made up of you and your selling skills, your company and their products and services, your prospect's personalities and their needs, and finally, your ability to overcome your competition. Selling can be very rewarding when you learn how to piece together the selling puzzle. Plus, with confidence in yourself, your products and services and the strength of your company backing, you will become a very formidable professional salesperson.

The goal of this book is for you to:

1. Understand that professional selling is an art and not a science.

2. Realize that successful selling is based on common sense, ethics and keeping things SIMPLE.

3. Learn how to apply the guidelines and proven techniques of successful professional selling.

4. Know and utilize more of the "Secrets Of How To Become A Professional Salesperson" than your competitors.

5. Be able to separate yourself as a true sales professional from the crowded field of other capable sales people.

6. Develop your selling talents and skills into your personal *art form* of selling.

7. Use your *mind* and *time management* wisely because they are the key resources to your success.

Learn and build on your selling experiences and gain knowledge from your successes as well as your losses. Although painful, many times you will learn more from your losses than from your wins. Always remember that you are ultimately the only one who has the greatest measure of control over your success as a professional salesperson.

Becoming a successful salesperson depends on how you think, relate to and approach selling in your **mind**. You must believe in yourself, your product and your company. You must have confidence in yourself and your selling abilities. Do not be boastful and prideful about wins because you will risk becoming overconfident. Do not let sales losses discourage you. You must have courage in the face of all adversities.

Accept your wins and losses with grace, honor and dignity. Strive to not become discouraged. A salesperson's greatest strengths are **a positive attitude, confidence** and **the will to succeed**. You may have bad days, weeks, months or even a bad year. However, keep working on the sales techniques and methods presented. Always try to keep moving forward. I know this is easier said than done. Strive to compartmentalize other business or personal issues that will distract you from your selling focus. Put them out of your mind when you are making your sales calls.

Whenever you are talking on the telephone or meeting with a customer or potential clients, try to always maintain an upbeat, positive, professional mental attitude. This is always the best approach, no matter what else may be happening in your life or career, because the account is most likely looking forward to meeting with you. You may be the first professional salesperson they are meeting with that is going to be able to satisfy their needs! Also, smile while you are talking to the account on the telephone. The account will *hear your smile*!

Take the extra time necessary to identify what the client's true needs and issues are that need to be resolved. Spend time *consulting with your accounts* so that they realize and understand all the options available to them. Put the extra effort into developing customized sales presentations, alternative solutions along with easy to understand pricing analysis. Your accounts will realize and appreciate the additional time you are spending to explain the details to them.

The extra effort you put forth on behalf of accounts will enable you to earn their trust and respect. They will also value you as a true sales consultant. When you begin working on this level, you will be developing your selling techniques into an *art form*. You will be selling with more genuine caring, confidence and enthusiasm. This type of consultative selling will pay you rich dividends, but you must invest the time and effort.

Remember to always be prepared and expect the unexpected. The unexpected will happen! When it does, be ready to be flexible, think on your feet, and quickly develop creative ideas of how to maintain control of the selling situation. Always have a positive attitude. Be professional, polite, respectful, ethical and honest in all matters. Be "open to possibilities" and "think outside of the box." Have perseverance in your selling campaigns. Be tenacious. Do not be afraid to fail. If you are afraid to try because of the possibility of failing, you will never succeed. Winners are never afraid to fail. Above all, use your common sense and keep the sales process SIMPLE!

Selling can be a very enjoyable and fulfilling career. Selling is really not that difficult. All it takes is common sense, diligence, determination, discipline and a willingness to learn something new every day. By practicing the successful selling techniques presented, you will be comfortable working with many different types of people and personalities.

The ultimate goal of this book is for you to be able to use these proven selling methods and techniques to take your professional selling abilities to the next higher level of professionalism. You will be able to develop a bond of trust and confidence between you and your prospects. Your confidence, enthusiasm and creativity will increase and you will find that you will begin to separate yourself from competitors. Your prospect will also notice the difference between you and your competition. Your accounts will respect you and will come to depend on and value you as their *consultative* partner.

Study, practice and use the selling techniques presented in this book. Do what comes natural to you. You will be pleased with just how many of these techniques you will remember and use automatically and naturally. Also, use your common sense and trust your instincts. Be ethical and honest at all times. Always maintain your character, principles, integrity and honor at the highest standards. The end result is that you will be able to separate yourself as a true sales professional from the crowded field of other capable sales people.

I hope that you have found these finer selling techniques, strategies and insights presented to be candid, easy to remember, understand, and implement. I trust that this information will serve you well and help you toward further developing and expanding your existing selling abilities and skills into your own personalized *art form* of selling!

Finally, I do wish you the best of success in your professional selling career. My goal for this book is that the knowledge and insights that I have acquired throughout my years of real world selling will be helpful and useful to those aspiring to be sales professionals. I trust this book will help you find that a career as a professional salesperson can be both exciting and rewarding. Good luck and good selling!

Printed in the United States
By Bookmasters